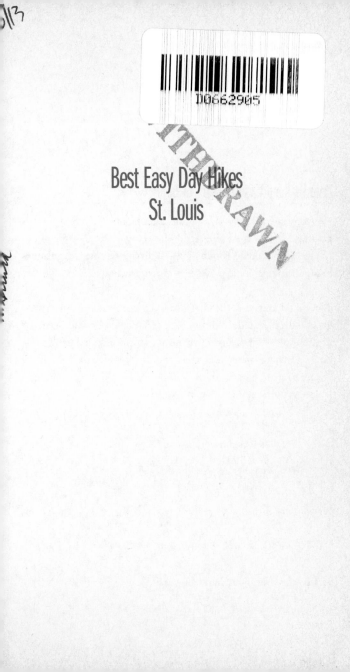

Best Easy Day Hikes
St. Louis

Help Us Keep This Guide Up to Date

Every effort has been made by the author and editors to make this guide as accurate and useful as possible. However, many things can change after a guide is published—trails are rerouted, regulations change, facilities come under new management, etc.

We would appreciate hearing from you concerning your experiences with this guide and how you feel it could be improved and kept up to date. While we may not be able to respond to all comments and suggestions, we'll take them to heart and we'll also make certain to share them with the author. Please send your comments and suggestions to the following address:

GPP
Reader Response/Editorial Department
P.O. Box 480
Guilford, CT 06437

Or you may e-mail us at:

editorial@GlobePequot.com

Thanks for your input, and happy trails!

Best Easy Day Hikes Series

Best Easy Day Hikes
St. Louis

JD Tanner and Emily Ressler

FALCONGUIDES

GUILFORD, CONNECTICUT
HELENA, MONTANA

AN IMPRINT OF GLOBE PEQUOT PRESS

FALCONGUIDES®

Copyright © 2011 by Morris Book Publishing, LLC

FalconGuides is an imprint of Morris Book Publishing, LLC.
Falcon, FalconGuides, and Outfit Your Mind are trademarks
of Morris Book Publishing, LLC.

Maps by Mapping Specialists © Morris Book Publishing LLC
TOPO! Explorer software and SuperQuad source maps courtesy of
National Geographic Maps. For information about TOPO! Explorer,
TOPO!, and Nat Geo Maps products, go to www.topo.com or www
.natgeomaps.com.

Project editor: Julie Marsh
Layout artist: Kevin Mak

Library of Congress Cataloging-in-Publication Data
Tanner, J. D.
  Best easy day hikes, St. Louis / J. D. Tanner and Emily Ressler.
    p. cm. — (FalconGuides)
  ISBN 978-0-7627-6354-2 (alk. paper)
  1. Hiking—Missouri—Saint Louis—Guidebooks. 2. Hiking—Mis-
souri—Saint Louis Region—Guidebooks. 3. Saint Louis (Mo.)—Guide-
books. 4. Saint Louis Region (Mo.)—Guidebooks. I. Ressler, Emily.
II. Title.
  GV199.42.M82S756 2011
  917.78'6604—dc22

                                           2010042882

Printed in the United States of America
10 9 8 7 6 5 4 3 2 1

Contents

The Hikes

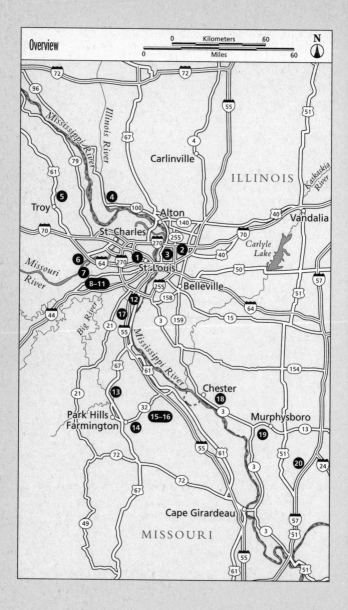

Acknowledgments

Special thanks to all the land managers who patiently answered our questions, pointed us toward the very best trails, and carefully reviewed the trail descriptions for this guide. We would also like to thank Ashley, Arnie, and Aspen for accompanying us on many of the trails in and around St. Louis; your company, humor, and enthusiasm were very much appreciated. Finally, we would like to thank all our friends at FalconGuides, particularly Max Phelps, Scott Adams, Jessica Haberman, and Julie Marsh, for their support and encouragement and for making a book out of our rough manuscript.

Introduction

When one thinks of "the best" hiking destinations in the United States, St. Louis, Missouri, may not be at the top of too many lists. Luckily, St. Louis–area residents, and now *you,* know better. The rolling hills of the Ozarks, the towering bluffs along the many rivers, the woodland bottoms and floodplains, and glacier-carved southern Illinois create a diverse backdrop for the hikes presented in this book.

This guide lists easy, moderate, and more challenging hikes within 100 miles of the St. Louis Metropolitan Area. Some of the hikes can be found within the city of St. Louis; others are located just south of the city in the northern Ozarks. A few more can be found just across the Mississippi River in southern Illinois.

The city of St. Louis was founded in 1764 by French traders, and at one time it was the fourth-largest city in the United States. Today the greater St. Louis area population is pushing almost three million people. The city boasts attractions like the Gateway Arch; the confluence of the Missouri, Illinois, and Mississippi Rivers; and of course the renowned Cardinals baseball team.

The Ozarks extend south and west from St. Louis throughout southern Missouri into northern Arkansas, eastern Oklahoma, and southeastern Kansas. Ecologically diverse, hilly, and sometimes rugged, southern Illinois not only offers great hiking but also provides many opportunities for canoeing, rock climbing, horseback riding, and much, much more.

Featured in the pages of this book are twenty of the best easy day hikes in and around the St. Louis area. We have done our best to include a little something for everyone. Hikes for families, for bird watching, for scenic views, and for pets have all been included and should be considered an introduction to the area and a starting point to continue your explorations.

The Nature of St. Louis

St. Louis–area trails range from rugged and hilly to flat and paved. Hikes in this guide cover a little bit of everything. While by definition a best easy day hike is not strenuous and poses little danger to the traveler, knowing a few details about the nature of the St. Louis area will only enhance your explorations.

Weather

Have you ever heard the expression "If you don't like the weather, just wait five minutes?" Well, people in St. Louis say it too.

The weather in the St. Louis area consists of a mild spring, ranging from cool to warm and muggy and typically wet. Trail conditions can be quite muddy during spring, especially for hikes that are in or near floodplains. The biggest concern for spring weather in St. Louis is the chance of thunderstorms, hail, or tornadoes.

Storms still pose a threat in early summer, but as summer progresses the weather tends to be less wet and sometimes very hot and almost always humid. Hikers who choose to get out in mid- to late summer might consider early-morning hikes, as high temperatures and humidity usually set in by midmorning.

Fall can be downright gorgeous in St. Louis. Daytime temperatures in the low to mid 70s along with the fall foliage can equal some amazingly scenic hikes. Fall hiking cannot be encouraged enough.

St. Louis has its fair share of cold and snowy days in winter, but if you don't mind having no leaves on the trees, winter can be a very enjoyable time to hike here. Winter hikers will get more views of the rolling Ozarks and will typically enjoy the trails almost all to themselves.

Ideal times for hiking in St. Louis are early to late spring and mid to late fall. Mix in the handful of cool days in summer and warm winter days, and you can expect to enjoy many ideal hiking days per year in St. Louis.

Hazards

There are few hazards to be aware of and prepare for when hiking in the St. Louis area.

Poison ivy might be the most common and most annoying issue hikers will come across while hiking in and around St. Louis. Poison ivy has been found in every county in Missouri. It can grow as a woody shrub, up to 6 feet high, or as a vine that clings to other trees and shrubs.

It is estimated that 50 to 70 percent of people experience a physical reaction after coming in contact with the plant. While the old expression "Leaves of three, let it be" is good advice to follow, there are several other three-leaf plants growing in the St. Louis area. Educate yourself about poison ivy before hitting the trail.

Poison ivy can be found year-round on almost every hike in this book.

Ticks are most abundant in St. Louis during spring and summer. There are many different types of ticks, but the two most common in Missouri are the Lone Star tick and the American dog tick. Ticks have been known to carry, and occasionally spread to humans, ailments such as Lyme disease, Rocky Mountain spotted fever, and tularemia.

Ticks are no reason to avoid hiking in the spring and summer seasons. To protect yourself, wear lighter-colored clothing to help detect ticks, wear long pants tucked into your hiking boots and a long-sleeved shirt, use repellent that is proven effective toward ticks, periodically check for ticks during your hike, and do a complete body check on yourself and pet after every hike.

During spring and summer, ticks can be found on every hike in this book.

Mosquitoes come in fifty different species in Missouri and Illinois. The most common concern with mosquitoes is the West Nile virus. It is estimated that only 1 percent of mosquitoes carry the West Nile virus and that only 1 percent of people bitten will actually contract the virus.

Like ticks, mosquitoes should not be a reason to avoid hiking in spring or summer. Hikers simply need to be aware and be prepared. For protection against mosquitoes, use insect repellent, wear long pants and a long-sleeved shirt, avoid hiking at dawn or dusk, and don't wear perfume or cologne when hiking.

Mosquitoes can be found on every hike in this book and can be quite abundant on the hikes located near floodplains.

Venomous snakes. Most of the snakes in the St. Louis area are harmless. However, hikers should be aware that several species of venomous snakes do inhabit the area.

Your chances of being bitten by a venomous snake in the United States are very, very low. Fewer than 8,000 people are bitten in the United States each year by venomous snakes, most while trying to handle or kill the snake, and fewer than five of those people die.

Missouri is home to five species of venomous snakes: The Osage copperhead, western cottonmouth (water moccasin), timber rattlesnake, eastern Massasauga rattlesnake (swamp rattler), and western pygmy rattlesnake (ground rattler) can all be found in or near the St. Louis area. The Osage copperhead and timber rattlesnake are the two venomous snakes hikers are most likely to encounter.

Venomous snakes in the St. Louis area are pit vipers that can be recognized by their "arrow-shaped" heads. Three of the five venomous snake species in Missouri are rattlesnakes and can be easily identified by the rattling noise they make when they feel threatened.

To protect against snakebite, wear protective footwear and keep an eye on the ground as you hike. Never place hands under rocks or logs, and never attempt to handle or kill any snakes you encounter.

Other Hazards
Other hazards you may encounter while hiking in the St. Louis area include drop-offs along bluffs, lightening, tornadoes, and heat-related illnesses.

Be Prepared

"Be prepared." The Boy Scouts say it, Leave No Trace says it, and the best outdoors people say it. Being prepared won't completely keep you out of harm's way when outdoors, but it will minimize the chances of finding yourself there. Here are some things to consider:

- Familiarize yourself with the basics of first aid (bites, stings, sprains, and breaks). Carry a first-aid kit, and know how to use it.

- Hydrate! No matter where or when you are hiking, always carry water with you. A standard is two liters per person per day.

- Be prepared to treat water on longer hikes. It is not safe to drink directly from rivers and streams in the St. Louis area. Iodine tablets are small, light, and easy to carry.

- Carry these "Ten Essentials" in your backpack: map, compass, sunglasses and sunscreen, extra food and water, extra clothes, headlamp/flashlight, first-aid kit, fire starter, matches, and knife.

- Pack your cell phone (set on vibrate) as a safety backup.

- Keep an eye on the kids. Give each child a whistle to blow in case he or she gets separated from you.

- Bring a leash, doggie waste bags, and extra water for your pet.

Learn as much as you can about the area you will be visiting. These guidelines plus being aware of the weather forecast, trail conditions, and water availability before you head out will help ensure a successful trip.

Leave No Trace

This hiking guide will take you to historical sites, conservation areas, national natural landmarks, and many other places of natural and cultural significance. The importance of Leave No Trace hiking cannot be stressed enough.

Do your best to stick to official trails so that you do not inadvertently trample sensitive vegetation. Be prepared to pack out everything you bring with you, and consider carrying out trash others may have left behind.

Be extra careful when visiting sites of historical and natural importance. Leave everything as you found it, and never remove artifacts from these sensitive areas.

Consider your impact on wildlife as you visit their homes. Feeding wildlife is unhealthy for the animals and dangerous for people.

Respect other visitors by keeping your pets on a leash, stepping to the side of the trail to allow others to pass, and keeping noise to a minimum.

For more information on enjoying the outdoors responsibly, visit the Leave No Trace Center for Outdoor Ethics at www.LNT.org.

Land Management

The following agencies manage the public lands where the hikes in this book are located. Contact them with any additional questions or concerns you have before visiting:

City of St. Louis Department of Parks, Recreation, and Forestry
5600 Clayton Rd.
St. Louis, MO 63110
http://stlouis.missouri.org/citygov/parks

Illinois Historic Preservation Agency
www.illinoishistory.gov
e-mail: HPA.info@illinois.gov

Illinois Department of Natural Resources
www.dnr.illinois.gov

Missouri Department of Natural Resources
P.O. Box 176
Jefferson City, MO 65102
(573) 751-3443; (800) 361-4827
www.dnr.mo.gov

Missouri Department of Conservation
St. Louis Regional Office
2360 Hwy. D
St. Charles, MO 63304
(636) 441-4554
http://mdc.mo.gov

St. Louis County Parks
41 South Central
Clayton, MO 63105
(314) 615-4386
www.co.st-louis.mo.us/parks/

Keep in mind that between the time this book was published and the time that you are reading it, some land management rules and regulations may have changed. Contact the appropriate agency for updated information about the area you plan to visit.

How to Use This Guide

This guide is designed to be simple and easy to use. Each hike is described with a map and summary information that delivers the trail's vital statistics, including distance and type (loop, lollipop, or out-and-back), difficulty, park hours, fees and permits, canine compatibility, and trail contacts. Directions to the trailhead are also provided, along with a general description of what you'll see along the way. A detailed route finder (Miles and Directions) sets forth mileages between significant landmarks along the trail.

How the Hikes Were Chosen

This guide describes trails that are accessible to every hiker, whether a visitor or a local resident. The hikes are no longer than 9 miles round-trip, and most are considerably shorter. They range in difficulty from flat excursions perfect for a family outing to more challenging treks in the rolling hills of the Ozarks.

While these trails are among the best, keep in mind that nearby trails, sometimes in the same park or in a neighboring open space, may offer options better suited to your needs. We've selected hikes in the immediate St. Louis Metropolitan Area, southern Illinois, and the northern Ozarks. Wherever your starting point, you'll find a great easy day hike nearby.

Selecting a Hike

These are all easy hikes, but *easy* is a relative term. Some would argue that no hike involving any kind of climbing is easy, but climbs are a fact of life in the St. Louis area.

Easy hikes are generally short and flat, taking no longer than an hour to complete.

Moderate hikes involve increased distance and relatively mild changes in elevation and will take one to two hours to complete.

More challenging hikes feature some steep stretches, greater distances, and generally take longer than two hours to complete.

Keep in mind that what you think is easy is entirely dependent on your level of fitness and the adequacy of your gear (primarily shoes). Use the trail's length as a gauge of its relative difficulty—even if climbing is involved, it won't be too strenuous if the hike is less than 1 mile long. If you are hiking with a group, select a hike that's appropriate for the least fit and prepared in your party.

Approximate hiking times are based on the assumption that on flat ground, most walkers average 2 miles per hour. Adjust that rate by the steepness of the terrain and your level of fitness (subtract time if you're an aerobic animal; add time if you're hiking with kids), and you have a ballpark hiking duration. Be sure to add more time if you plan to picnic or take part in other activities like bird watching or photography.

Trail Finder

Best Hikes for Birders

Best Hikes with Children

Best Hikes with Dogs

Best Hikes for Great Views

Best Hikes for Nature Lovers

Best Hikes for History Buffs

Map Legend

═══⟨55⟩═══	Interstate Highway
──⟨67⟩──	U.S. Highway
──⟨4⟩──	State Highway
────────	Local Road
═══════	Unpaved Road
┼─┼─┼─┼	Railroad
▬▬▬▬▬▬	Featured Trail
─ ─ ─ ─ ─	Trail
─ ·─ ·─ ·─	County Line
─ ·· ─ ·· ─	State Line
⌇	River/Creek
▭	Local/State Park
▭	National Park / Forest
⛵	Boat Launch
⌣	Bridge
▲	Campground
🅿	Parking
🏕	Picnic Area
■	Point of Interest/Structure
🚻	Restroom
‖‖‖‖	Steps
⟲	Spring
○	Town
⓫	Trailhead
◈	Viewpoint/Overlook
❷	Visitor/Information Center

1 Forest Park: Heels Path

Located in the heart of St. Louis, Forest Park is one of the largest urban parks in the United States. This easy trail forms a loop around the perimeter of the park and passes several of the city's most popular attractions, including the St. Louis Science Center, the St. Louis Zoo, and the Missouri History Museum, all of which are available to the public free of charge.

Distance: 5.7-mile loop
Approximate hiking time: 3 hours
Difficulty: Moderate due to length
Best season: Year-round
Park hours: Open 24 hours
Other trail users: Joggers and bikers
Canine compatibility: Leashed dogs permitted
Fees and permits: None

Maps: USGS Clayton; detailed trail map and brochure available at the visitor center
Trail contacts: Forest Park Forever, Dennis & Judith Jones Visitor and Education Center, 5595 Grand Dr., Forest Park, St. Louis, MO 63112; (314) 367-7275; www.forestparkforever.org
Special considerations: Watch for traffic when crossing park roads.

Finding the trailhead: From downtown St. Louis take I-64 West/US 40 West to the exit for Kingshighway Boulevard. Take Kingshighway Boulevard north and turn left (west) onto Lindell Boulevard. Turn south (left) onto Cricket Drive and then right onto Grand Drive. The Dennis & Judith Jones Visitor and Education Center is ahead on the right. There is a large parking lot located across the street (south) of the center. The trail begins on the north end of the visitor center. GPS: N38 38.604 / W90 16.957

The Hike

Dedicated in 1876, the 1,371-acre Forest Park is one of the oldest and largest urban parks in the United States. With more than 18,000 trees, Forest Park provides ideal habitat for many species of birds, including five species of woodpeckers, several species of owls, and the iconic northern cardinal, which is the mascot for the city's baseball team. Wildlife is also abundant in the park, and it is not uncommon for visitors to see squirrels, foxes, raccoons, muskrats, woodchucks, and chipmunks.

The trail begins at the north end of the Dennis & Judith Jones Visitor and Education Center. The center offers water, restrooms, day lockers, and the Forest Park Cafe. It also houses the Missouri Department of Conservation and Forest Park Forever, a nonprofit organization working to restore, maintain, and sustain Forest Park. Visitor information is provided through the St. Louis Convention and Visitors Commission.

From the north end of the visitor center, the trail turns to the right (east), following the northern border of the park. After 0.2 mile the trail crosses Cricket Drive and continues east, crossing Union Drive (0.5 mile) and Grand Drive (0.8 mile) before reaching Round Lake.

The path continues south, passing Jefferson Lake to the east. Jefferson Lake offers good fishing for St. Louis anglers. More than twenty-five species of fish can be found in Forest Park, including rainbow trout, largemouth bass, bluegill, channel catfish, and white crappie.

At 1.0 mile come to a fork in the path; stay left to cross a bridge. At this point the walking path merges with the bike path and is shared by both users until the walking path

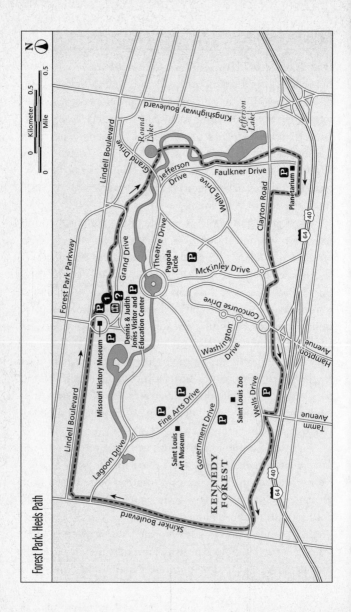

Forest Park: Heels Path

reemerges near Tamm Avenue. There are several portions of the path under construction in this area, so be aware of any detours.

Cross Clayton Road at 1.5 miles and skirt the James S. McDonnell Planetarium, which is connected to the St. Louis Science Center via a footbridge to the south. The St. Louis Science Center offers over 700 exhibits; general admission is free to the public. Pass the Science Park and the dinosaur replicas at 1.6 miles. From here the path turns to the right and follows the southern border of the park, crossing McKinley Drive (2.4 miles) and then using a pedestrian underpass to traverse Hampton Avenue at Concourse Drive (2.7 miles).

After traveling through the pedestrian underpass, the trail passes the St. Louis Zoo. Home to almost 23,000 animals from all over the world, the zoo offers free general admission and makes a fine addition to this hike. On the west end of the zoo parking lot, the trail crosses Tamm Avenue (3.3 miles).

At 3.8 miles cross Wells Drive and bear right (north), passing Kennedy Forest. Cross Lagoon Drive (4.5 miles); the path curves to the right (east) to follow the northern border of the park. At 5.4 miles come to the Missouri History Museum, another great St. Louis resource that is available to the public free of charge.

Just past the museum, the trail veers to the southeast to complete the loop at the Dennis & Judith Jones Visitor and Education Center.

Miles and Directions

0.0 Begin at the Dennis & Judith Jones Visitor and Education Center and head east.

0.2 Cross Cricket Drive and continue east.

0.5 Cross Union Drive and continue on the walking trail as it bends to the right (southeast).

0.8 Cross Grand Drive and continue southeast, passing Round Lake to the left (north).

1.0 Walking path merges with bike path; stay left at the fork and cross a bridge.

1.5 Cross Clayton Road and skirt the James S. McDonnell Planetarium.

1.6 Pass the Science Park and come to the dinosaur replicas.

2.4 Cross McKinley Drive and continue west.

2.7 Use the pedestrian underpass to traverse Hampton Avenue at Concourse Drive.

3.3 Cross Tamm Avenue and continue west on the walking path.

3.8 Cross Wells Drive and turn north.

4.5 Cross Lagoon Drive; the trail soon curves to the right (east).

5.4 Come to the Missouri History Museum.

5.7 Return to the Dennis & Judith Jones Visitor and Education Center.

2 Cahokia Mounds State Historic Site: Nature/Culture Trail

This easy stroll explores the remains of the most sophisticated prehistoric Native American civilization north of Mexico. Weaving its way around ancient mounds, this loop trail offers visitors an up-close look at the mysterious and ancient city known as Cahokia.

Distance: 4.0-mile loop
Approximate hiking time: 2 hours
Difficulty: Easy due to flat terrain
Best season: Fall through spring
Park hours: Open 8 a.m. to dusk
Other trail users: None
Canine compatibility: Leashed dogs permitted
Fees and permits: None required (donation suggested)

Maps: USGS Monks Mound; interpretive trail map available at the visitor center
Trail contacts: Cahokia Mounds State Historic Site, 30 Ramey St., Collinsville IL 62234; (618) 346-5160; www.cahokia mounds.org
Special considerations: Watch for traffic when crossing roads.

Finding the trailhead: From St. Louis take I-55 North/I-70 East/ US 40 East toward Illinois. After 6.7 miles, take exit 6 and turn right onto IL 111. Turn left after 0.2 mile onto Collinsville Road and drive 1.9 miles. Turn right onto Ramey Street and arrive at the visitor center and trailhead parking. GPS: N38 39.309 / W90 3.574

The Hike

The hike begins on the northwest corner of the visitor center, a great resource and a recommended stop for anyone wanting to learn about this unique historic site. The visitor

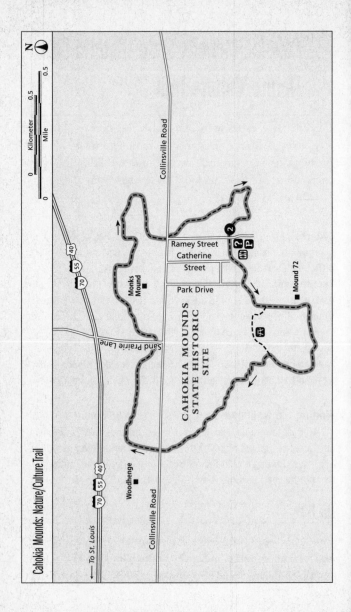

Cahokia Mounds: Nature/Culture Trail

center offers restrooms, water, vending machines, and a gift shop. It houses a museum, which describes prehistoric Cahokia and brings to life the area you are about to hike through.

In the gift shop you can purchase or borrow the *Nature/Culture Hike Guidebook,* an in-depth interpretive guide that describes the thirty-two markers you will see along this hike. The visitor center also allows guests to rent iPod Touch players for an audiovisual tour of three interpretive trails.

This hike is all about seeing the famous "mounds" of Cahokia. There are over one hundred mounds in the area, and this path will lead you past many of them. The mounds are made entirely of soil, which was transported by the people of Cahokia in baskets to the site between around A.D. 700 and 1400. These mounds served several purposes for the Cahokians, including bases for ceremonial structures, location markers, and burial sites for important people of the time.

The largest mound you will encounter on this hike is Mound 38, known as Monks Mound (2.7 miles), which is over 100 feet tall and covers some fourteen acres of land. Mound 72 (0.4 mile) is the site for almost 300 ceremonial and sacrificial burials. At 1.7 miles come to Woodhenge, a reconstructed sunrise-horizon calendar. Constructed from cedar posts and 410 feet in diameter, the circular calendar marked the seasons and important dates for the Cahokians.

Despite being located in a heavily used area (I-55/70 and busy Collinsville Road cut across the site toward the northern border), the site is rich in natural history. Visitors are likely to encounter wildlife on the trail, including white-tailed deer, gray squirrel, red fox, and eastern chipmunk.

Additionally, there are many examples of prairie grasses, flowering plants, and trees, many of which were staples in the everyday lives of the Cahokians.

Miles and Directions

0.0 From the visitor center follow the paved walkway to the left (southwest). The trail is marked with blue arrows.

0.4 Pass Mound 72 (to the east) and reach the end of the paved portion of the trail. Continue south, and then follow the blue arrows as the trail turns to the west then north.

1.3 Come to a connector trail branching to the right (marked with a white arrow), which returns to the visitor center. Stay left (northwest), following the blue arrow to continue on the trail.

1.7 Cross Collinsville Road and continue north past Woodhenge.

2.3 Cross Sand Prairie Lane and continue east-northeast.

2.7 Reach the north end of Monks Mound; continue east.

3.4 Cross Collinsville Road again and continue south toward the visitor center.

3.9 Come to a connector trail, marked with a white arrow. Turn right (northwest) onto the connector trail to return to the visitor center.

4.0 Arrive back at the visitor center.

3 Horseshoe Lake State Park: Walkers Island Trail

This easy and flat hike forms a loop around the perimeter of Walkers Island. Just minutes from St. Louis, Walkers Island provides rich habitat for birds and other wildlife.

Distance: 3.7-mile loop
Approximate hiking time: 2 hours
Difficulty: Easy; flat terrain
Best season: Year-round
Park hours: Sunrise to 10 p.m.
Other trail users: None
Canine compatibility: Leashed dogs permitted
Fees and permits: None
Maps: USGS Monks Mound; interpretive trail map available at the park office

Trail contacts: Horseshoe Lake State Park, 3321 Hwy. 111, Granite City IL 62040; (618) 931-0270
Special considerations: Sections of the trail may be flooded following periods of rainfall. Hunting is permitted in the area during various seasons. Contact the park office for current trail conditions and seasonal closures.

Finding the trailhead: From St. Louis take I-55 North/I-70 East/ US 40 East toward Illinois. After 6.7 miles, take exit 6 and turn left onto IL 111. Continue for 3.1 miles to the park entrance on the left. From the park entrance, follow the main road past the park office on the left and cross the causeway. At 0.8 mile from the entrance, reach the parking area and picnic shelter. The trail is located across the road (north) from the picnic shelter and parking area. GPS: N38 41.709 / W90 4.480

The Hike

Despite being minutes from downtown St. Louis, Horseshoe Lake State Park feels far removed from city life. The park itself offers many recreational opportunities, including camping, hiking, hunting, fishing, and bird watching. Located in a low floodplain, the park provides perfect habitat for many species of wildlife. A birding checklist is available at the park office and will clue hikers in on which birds they can expect to see on Walkers Island. Restrooms and water are available at the park office and at the campground.

The trail begins just north of the trailhead parking area. Follow the slightly worn path through the grass as it heads north toward the shore of Horseshoe Lake. The trailhead is marked with a sign indicating the start of the hiking trail. The obvious trail continues northeast following the shoreline. As you hike through this wooded section of the trail, you will notice many species of trees, including hackberry, which provides a valuable source of food for birds and wildlife.

After hiking 0.6 mile, come to an open area; the trail turns sharply to the left. This is a great place to watch for wood ducks and other diving ducks that prefer the open water.

The trail continues south, passing through old farm fields and the Hardwood Pond area at 1.3 miles. Both areas provide great habitat for wildlife. Look for white-tailed deer, coyote, opossum, red fox, box turtle, and beaver. As you reach the southern end of the island, the trail curves to the left (east), passing the campground (2.5 miles) and returns to the trailhead parking area via the island's eastern shore.

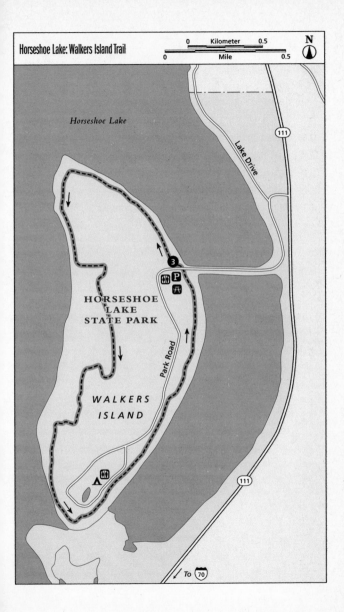

Horseshoe Lake: Walkers Island Trail

Horseshoe Lake

111

Lake Drive

3

HORSESHOE
LAKE
STATE PARK

Park Road

WALKERS
ISLAND

111

To 70

Miles and Directions

0.0 From the trailhead parking area and picnic shelter, walk across the park road and follow the faint trail north as it heads toward the shore of Horseshoe Lake.

0.2 Reach the wooden sign that reads HIKING TRAIL START.

0.6 The trail turns sharply to the left (south).

1.3 Pass through the Hardwood Pond area.

2.5 Pass campground on the left (west) and continue north, following the eastern shore of the island.

3.7 Return to the trailhead parking area and picnic shelter.

4 Pere Marquette State Park: Goat Cliff Trail

Known for its abundant winter eagle population, Pere Marquette State Park has something for every type of outdoor enthusiast. This short but challenging hike offers some of the best views in the park.

Distance: 1.7-mile loop
Approximate hiking time: 1 hour
Difficulty: More challenging due to demanding climb
Best season: Spring through fall
Park hours: Open 24 hours; hikers should be off trails by sunset
Other trail users: None
Canine compatibility: Leashed dogs permitted

Fees and permits: None
Maps: USGS Brussels; park maps available at visitor center
Trail contacts: Pere Marquette State Park, Route 100, P.O. Box 158, Grafton IL 62037; (618) 786-3323
Special considerations: Mosquitoes and poison ivy are common in warmer months.

Finding the trailhead: From downtown St. Louis take I-70 West to exit 243A (Goodfellow Boulevard). Turn right (east) onto Goodfellow Boulevard and drive 2.3 miles to a roundabout; turn right off the roundabout northbound onto MO 367 North/Lewis & Clark Boulevard. Take MO 367 North/Lewis & Clark Boulevard/US 67 North for 13.4 miles into Illinois and bear left onto US 67 North/Landmarks Boulevard/Great River Road. Travel 0.9 mile to the intersection with IL 100/W. Broadway St./McAdams Pkwy. Turn left onto IL 100 and continue for 20.9 miles to Pere Marquette State Park entrance. Continue 0.5 mile from the park entrance on IL 100 before turning right onto Scenic Drive and then left into the visitor center and trailhead parking area. The trailhead is located on the northwest corner of the parking area. GPS: N38 58.413 / W90 32.660

The Hike

Except for the hottest of summer days, Pere Marquette State Park is a pleasant trip for outdoor enthusiasts looking for great camping, hiking, biking, horseback riding, fishing, and bird watching. During fall, visitors are treated to an array of colors as the leaves change. Throughout the winter months, it is common to see the bald eagles that make their winter home along the Illinois River. In spring, wildflowers and wildlife are in abundance. Even summer can be a pleasant time to visit, since much of the park enjoys the shaded cover of the woodland canopy.

Although Pere Marquette State Park offers several great hiking trails, the Goat Cliff Trail is perhaps the most scenic. It makes a great place to begin your explorations in the park.

From the northwest corner of the parking area, locate the obvious dirt trail heading north. Follow this trail as it briefly parallels IL 100 before it begins to ascend a moderate ridge. At 0.2 mile come to Twin Springs and note the oddly angled rocks that represent the Cap au Grès Fault. Take a moment to appreciate the fact that you are standing on a fault line, then continue north through the mixed woodland of sugar maples, oaks, and hickories.

At 0.7 reach a scenic overlook, which allows a good view of the farm valley to the northwest. From the overlook the trail turns to the southeast and follows the back side of the ridgeline. Come to a fork in the trail at 0.9 mile. Bear right onto the smaller trail to visit the Goat Cliff Hill Prairie Overlook (0.94 mile), which is part of the McAdams Peak Hill Prairie Natural Area. The trail rejoins the Goat Cliff

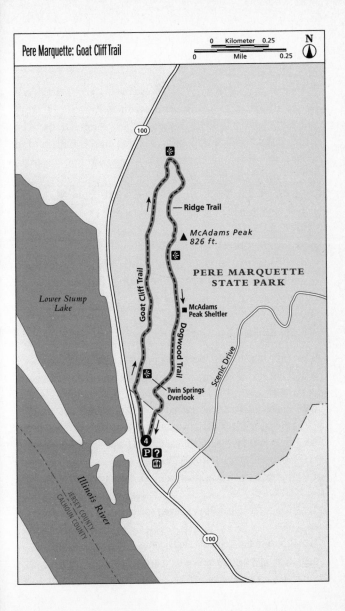

Pere Marquette: Goat Cliff Trail

0 Kilometer 0.25
0 Mile 0.25

N

State Route 100

Ridge Trail

▲ McAdams Peak
826 ft.

Goat Cliff Trail

PERE MARQUETTE
STATE PARK

Lower Stump
Lake

Dogwood Trail

■ McAdams
Peak Sheltler

Scenic Drive

Twin Springs
Overlook

4
P ?

Illinois River

JERSEY COUNTY
CALHOUN COUNTY

100

Trail at 1.0 mile, just before the McAdams Peak Shelter, which offers another pretty place to take in views of the Illinois River.

Several trails converge at McAdams Peak Shelter, and hikers wishing to extend their trip can follow the Hickory Trail east, which links to several other, longer trails. The visitor center offers a trail map that lists all the trails within the park and should be consulted before extending this hike.

The most direct route back to the trailhead parking area is the Ridge Trail, which heads south from McAdams Peak Shelter for 0.2 mile until it converges with the Dogwood Trail at 1.3 miles. You can follow either leg of the Dogwood Trail back to the trailhead parking area, but the leg that forks to the right (southwest) offers a final scenic overlook. At 1.5 miles turn right (south) and return to the trailhead parking area at 1.7 miles.

Miles and Directions

0.0 From the trailhead follow the obvious path north.

0.2 Come to Twin Springs and the Cap au Grès Fault; continue north.

0.7 Reach a scenic overlook and then follow the trail as it turns sharply to the south.

0.9 Bear right (southwest) at the fork and take small side trail to Goat Cliff Prairie Overlook.

1.0 The side trail rejoins Goat Cliff Trail; continue south on the Goat Cliff Trail.

1.1 Reach McAdams Peak Shelter; continue south on the Ridge Trail.

1.3 Come to the Dogwood Trail and bear right (southwest).

1.5 Turn right (south) toward the parking area.

1.7 Return to the trailhead/visitor center parking area.

5 Cuivre River State Park: Lone Spring Trail

The Lone Spring Trail provides an interesting trek through a woodland of shagbark hickory and white, black, and northern red oaks. Lone Spring appears from under a shelf of limestone and offers hikers a calm spot to relax and take in the sights and sounds of this unique park.

Distance: 5.8-mile loop

Approximate hiking time: 3 hours

Difficulty: More challenging due to length

Best season: Fall through spring

Park hours: Open 24 hours

Other trail users: None

Canine compatibility: Leashed dogs permitted

Fees and permits: None

Maps: USGS Okete; park map available at visitor center

Trail contacts: Cuivre River State Park, 678 SR 147, Troy, MO 63379; (636) 528-7247; www .mostateparks.com/cuivre.htm

Special considerations: Use caution when crossing park roads. Ticks and poison ivy are common during summer.

Finding the trailhead: From St. Louis take I-64 West/US 40 West for about 40 miles until the road becomes US 61 North. Continue on US 61 North for 14.8 miles to the MO 47 exit (toward Troy). Turn right onto MO 47 and drive 3.1 miles. Turn left onto MO 147 and continue for 1.8 miles to the visitor center. At the visitor center turn right onto Lincoln Hills Road; drive 5 miles through the park until the road meets MO KK. The parking area is to the right. The trailhead is located across MO KK. GPS: N39 3.948 / W90 55.997

The Hike

Located northwest of St. Louis, Cuivre River State Park stands in contrast to other natural areas located in northern Missouri. Its landscape is comparable in many ways to that of the Ozarks, and the cave, springs, sinkholes, rocky creeks, and dramatic limestone bluffs found here make it a worthy destination for any hiker. The visitor center offers displays on the area's cultural and natural history, as well as restrooms, water, and park maps.

From the trailhead parking area, cross MO KK and locate the Lone Spring Trail about 30 yards to the left (northwest). A sign alerts visitors that they are entering the Northwoods Wild Area, and a smaller sign marks the beginning of the Lone Spring Trail. Enter the woods here and turn left (west) onto Lone Spring Trail. After 0.3 mile reach the trailhead register. Sign in before turning right (northwest) to continue on Lone Spring Trail.

At 1.3 miles come to a spur trail that forks left and leads to Lone Spring and a wooden bench, which offers an ideal place to relax. After taking in the sights of Lone Spring, follow the spur trail back to Lone Spring Trail and continue northeast, passing a sinkhole on the right. Avoid the spur trail at 1.6 miles, which leads to a backcountry campsite; follow the yellow arrow east to continue on the Lone Spring Trail.

Reach a spur trail at 2.5 miles that heads north for 0.5 mile to Shady-Eighty Ranch Lake. This spur offers a nice side trip and primitive camping options.

At 3.0 miles cross MO KK and continue to the Lone Spring Trail–South Loop. The trail branching to the west leads back to the trailhead parking area and can be used to

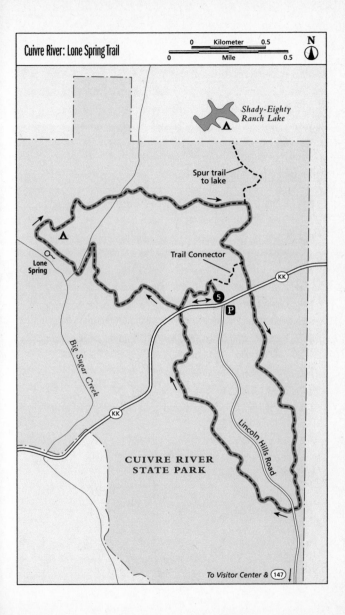

Cuivre River: Lone Spring Trail

Kilometer

Mile

N

Shady-Eighty
Ranch Lake

Spur trail
to lake

Trail Connector

KK

5

P

Lone
Spring

Big Sugar Creek

KK

Lincoln Hills Road

CUIVRE RIVER
STATE PARK

To Visitor Center & 147

shorten your hike. Enter a grove of eastern cedar after 4.0 miles. Shortly after, cross Lincoln Hills Road and follow the trail as it turns to the northwest.

After 5.3 miles cross MO KK for the final time. Follow the trail into the woods and turn right (east) at the trailhead register, following the trail back to the trailhead parking area.

Miles and Directions

0.0 From the trailhead enter the woods and turn left (west) onto Lone Spring Trail.

0.3 Come to the trailhead register. After signing in, turn right (northwest) to continue on the Lone Spring Trail.

1.3 Reach a spur trail branching to the left. Go left to visit Lone Spring, or stay right to continue on the Lone Spring Trail.

1.6 Come to a spur trail leading to the backcountry camping area; stay straight (east) to continue on the main trail.

2.5 Pass the spur trail, branching to the north, for Shady-Eighty Ranch Lake.

3.0 Continue southeast and cross MO KK.

4.0 Enter grove of eastern cedars.

4.1 Cross Lincoln Hills Road and continue on the trail as it turns to the northwest.

5.3 Cross MO KK and follow the trail into the woods. Turn right (east) at the trailhead register.

5.8 Return to trailhead.

6 Weldon Spring Conservation Area: Lewis Trail

This loop hike takes you through the Weldon Spring Conservation Area. Towering limestone bluffs offering excellent views of the Missouri River, abundant wildlife, and easy access from St. Louis combine to make for an ideal day trip.

Distance: 8.0-mile loop
Approximate hiking time: 4 hours
Difficulty: More challenging due to length and demanding climbs
Best season: Fall through spring
Park hours: 4 a.m.–10 p.m.
Other trail users: None
Canine compatibility: Leashed dogs permitted
Fees and permits: None
Maps: USGS Weldon Spring; park map and brochure available at the visitor center

Trail contacts: Missouri Department of Conservation, St. Louis Regional Office, 2360 Hwy. D, St. Charles, MO 63304; (636) 441-4554
Special considerations: Use caution near steep bluffs. Mosquitoes can be very abundant during warmer seasons. Hunting is permitted in the area during various seasons; contact the park office for details.

Finding the trailhead: From St. Louis drive almost 29 miles on I-64 West/US 40 West to exit 10 (MO 94). Turn left onto MO 94 West and drive 2.4 miles to the Weldon Spring Wildlife Area parking and Lewis and Clark trailheads. GPS: N38 41.445 / W90 43.452

The Hike

Located in St. Charles County, the 8,359-acre Weldon Spring Conservation Area offers a variety of natural features,

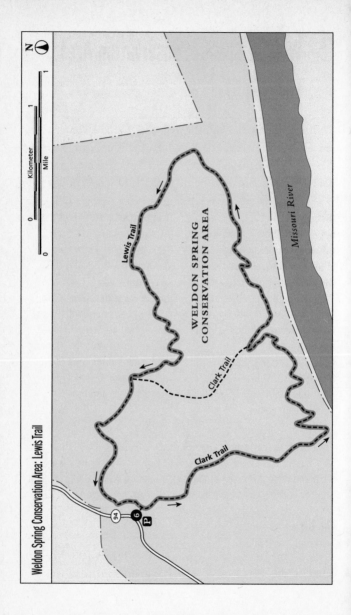

Weldon Spring Conservation Area: Lewis Trail

including large plots of forest, tall limestone bluffs, wetlands, glades, pastures, and some agricultural lands. This combination of habitats makes for a diverse collection of flora and fauna, despite the area's close proximity to the city. White-tailed deer, wild turkeys, raccoons, squirrels, foxes, and five-lined skinks (a type of lizard) are just some of the wild animals that flourish here. The southern border of the area is formed by the Missouri River. The Katy Trail, a 225-mile-long biking and walking trail, cuts across the southern portion of the conservation area.

Located next to the information kiosk, the Clark Trail and the Lewis Trail begin on the eastern end of the parking area. The trailhead is marked with a wooden sign for the CLARK TRAIL 5.3 MILES and the LEWIS TRAIL 8.2 MILES. Begin hiking north on the obvious path, passing eastern red cedar, roughleaf dogwood, honey locust, and eastern redbud trees. After 0.1 mile the trail forks; stay right (south), following the white arrow.

At 1.3 miles you gain sight of the Missouri River and come to an interpretive sign, which gives historical information on the Lewis and Clark expedition. Follow the trail as it turns sharply to the left (north).

After climbing a moderately steep ridge, pass several scenic overlooks at 2.2 miles. The impressive limestone bluffs tower above the Missouri River and the famous Katy Trail. From here the trail descends the ridge to a dry creek bottom (2.8 miles). Cross the creek and follow its bank to the intersection of the Clark and Lewis Trails at 2.9 miles. Stay right (east) to continue on the Lewis Trail. **(Option:** Turn left here for a 5.3-mile hike of about 3 hours.)

The trail follows an old fenceline (3.3 miles) along the bluffs before descending again via a series of mellow switchbacks through a mostly maple and oak forest. The trail crosses a small footbridge at 5.4 miles and then an access road at 5.6 miles.

At 6.4 miles the trail rejoins the Clark Trail, stay right (north) at this intersection to complete the loop. Cross another footbridge at 7.0 miles and continue southwest to the trailhead parking area.

Miles and Directions

0.0 Hike north from the parking lot to the combined Lewis and Clark Trails.

0.1 Reach a fork in the trail; turn right (south) to stay on the Lewis and Clark Trails. (The larger loop, our recommended hike, is the Lewis Trail; the smaller loop, the Clark Trail.)

1.3 Come to the Lewis and Clark interpretive sign. Follow the trail as it curves to the left (north).

2.2 After ascending a moderately steep ridge, come to a series of overlooks.

2.8 Cross a dry creek bottom.

2.9 Intersect with the Clark Trail; keep to the right (southeast) to stay on the Lewis Trail. **(Option:** Turn left [north] onto the Clark Trail for a 5.3-mile loop that takes about 3 hours to hike. Turn left onto the Lewis Trail at mile 6.4 below.)

3.3 Follow the trail as it parallels an old fenceline along limestone bluffs.

5.4 Cross a small footbridge.

5.6 Cross an access road.

6.4 Come to intersection with the Clark Trail; stay right (north) to complete the loop.

7.0 Cross a footbridge and continue southwest.

8.0 Return to trailhead parking area.

7 Dr. Edmund A. Babler Memorial State Park: Dogwood Trail

One of the more challenging hikes in Dr. Edmund A. Babler Memorial State Park, the Dogwood Trail offers nature lovers an interesting mix of forest habitats.

Distance: 2.2-mile loop
Approximate hiking time: 1 hour
Difficulty: Moderate due to modest elevation change
Best season: Year-round
Park hours: Apr–Oct, 7 a.m.–9 p.m.; Nov–Mar, 7 a.m.–6 p.m.
Other trail users: Equestrians on portions of the trail
Canine compatibility: Leashed dogs permitted

Fees and permits: None
Maps: USGS Eureka; park map available at the visitor center
Trail contacts: Dr. Edmund A. Babler Memorial State Park, 800 Guy Park Dr., Wildwood, MO 63005; (636) 458-3813; http: //mostateparks.com/babler.htm
Special considerations: Ticks, poison ivy, and mosquitoes are common in warmer months.

Finding the trailhead: From St. Louis take I-64 West/US 40 West for 23 miles to exit 16 (Long Road). After 1.4 miles turn right onto Wild Horse Creek Road/MO CC. Drive 3.1 miles before turning left onto MO 109. Continue for 0.7 mile and turn right onto Babler Park Drive. After 1.5 miles turn right onto the gated Guy Park Drive and continue straight to the visitor center. From the visitor center drive 1.5 miles on Guy Park Drive to the large parking area and trailhead. GPS: N38 37.369 / W90 41.870

The Hike

In 1938 Jacob and Henry Babler presented the State of Missouri with sixty-eight acres of hilly countryside as a way to commemorate their brother, Dr. Edmund A. Babler, a well-known and well-loved St. Louis surgeon. Since then the park has grown to 2,500 acres—a precious "green-space oasis" amidst the ever-growing suburbs of St. Louis County.

Visiting old-growth forests featuring white oak, eastern red cedar, sugar maple, walnut, dogwood, pawpaw, and redbud is a rare treat for park visitors so close to a major urban area. A favorite with bird-watchers, the park is home to many species of birds, including downy, redheaded, red-bellied, and pileated woodpeckers.

The Dogwood Trail is one of the best ways to experience the park's many natural treasures. This loop is the longest and most challenging, albeit still moderate, hiking trail in the park and provides a good overview of the flora and fauna found in the area. The hike is easily extended by adding the 1.8-mile Woodbine Trail, which shares the same trailhead, to the end of this hike.

On the northeast end of the parking area, locate the information kiosk, which marks the trailhead for both the Dogwood and the Woodbine Trails. Follow the Dogwood Trail, marked with green arrows, to the north through a typical Missouri hardwood forest. At 0.2 mile come the beginning/end of the loop portion of the Dogwood Trail and turn right (east).

At 0.5 mile the Dogwood Trail merges with an equestrian trail and becomes wider and rockier for 0.2 mile as it ascends the ridge. Near the top of the ridge, pass the stone Cochran Shelter and restroom. During the 1930s this site was built by groups from the Civilian Conservation Corps (CCC), which used the park as a base and constructed many of the roads, trails, and stone structures found here.

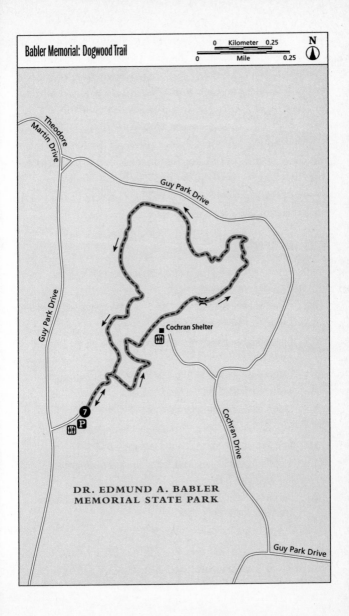

Babler Memorial: Dogwood Trail

0 Kilometer 0.25

0 Mile 0.25

N

Theodore Martin Drive

Guy Park Drive

Guy Park Drive

Cochran Shelter

7

P

Cochran Drive

DR. EDMUND A. BABLER
MEMORIAL STATE PARK

Guy Park Drive

At 1.1 miles come to a spur trail to the right, which leads to the Bates Picnic Area. Stay left (southwest) to continue on the Dogwood Trail. Briefly merge with an equestrian trail at 1.3 miles and then turn right at 1.4 miles to continue on the Dogwood Trail. At 1.5 miles the trail forks again; turn left (south) to stay on the Dogwood Trail.

After hiking 1.6 miles, enter a grove of eastern red cedars and cross a small footbridge, which leads you to a fork in the trail. Stay left to continue on the Dogwood Trail.

At 2.0 miles reach the end of the Dogwood Trail loop and return to the parking area.

Miles and Directions

0.0 From the trailhead hike north, following the green arrows for the Dogwood Trail.

0.2 Come to the loop portion of the hike; stay right (east).

0.5 Dogwood Trail merges briefly with an equestrian trail.

0.7 Stay right (northeast) at the fork to continue on the Dogwood Trail.

1.1 Reach the spur trail to Bates Picnic Area; stay left (southwest) to continue on the Dogwood Trail.

1.3 Merge onto an equestrian trail for 0.1 mile.

1.4 Stay right at the fork to continue on the Dogwood Trail.

1.5 Turn left (south) to stay on the Dogwood Trail.

1.6 Cross a footbridge and stay left at the fork to continue on the Dogwood Trail.

2.0 Reach to the end of the loop. Bear right (west) toward the trailhead and parking area.

2.2 Return to the trailhead and parking area.

Option: Continue on the Woodbine Trail (marked with blue arrows) for an additional 1.8 miles.

8 Rockwoods Reservation: Lime Kiln Loop Trail

This fine loop trail offers a peaceful and shaded trek though Rockwoods Reservation, one of the oldest conservation areas in the state of Missouri.

Distance: 2.8-mile loop
Approximate hiking time: 1.5 hours
Difficulty: Moderate due to modest climb
Best season: Year-round
Park hours: Open sunrise to half hour after sunset
Other trail users: None
Canine compatibility: Dogs not permitted

Fees and permits: None
Maps: USGS Eureka; park map available at the visitor center
Trail contacts: Rockwoods Reservation, 2751 Glencoe Rd., Glencoe, MO 63038; (636) 458-2236
Special considerations: Ticks and mosquitoes may be present in warmer months.

Finding the trailhead: From St. Louis take I-44 West for 25 miles to exit 264 (MO 109). Turn right onto MO 109 and drive 4 miles before turning left onto Woods Avenue and then right into Rockwoods Reservation on Glencoe Road. Continue 0.5 mile from the park entrance to the trailhead, located on the right. GPS: N38 33.482 / W90 39.113

The Hike

Established in 1938, Rockwoods Reservation consists of 1,880 acres of dense forests, streams, springs, caves, prairie grass, and limestone deposits. There are several trails in the

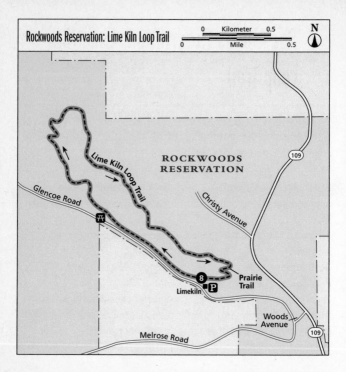

park. All are worthwhile, but the Lime Kiln Loop Trail offers a more challenging route through some of the best scenery in the area and makes a fantastic day trip just minutes from St. Louis.

Find the trailhead to the north of the small parking area; it is marked with a sign reading LIME KILN LOOP TRAIL 3¼ MILES. Just beyond this sign you will see a large limekiln, one of the oldest in the area. An interpretive sign explains the history of the lime kiln; turn left (northwest) here and follow the trail as it parallels Glencoe Road. At 0.3 mile rock-hop across a small stream and continue northwest.

At 1.0 mile cross a drainage and follow the trail as it turns to the northwest and begins a moderately steep ascent up the ridge. A bench at the top of this ridge (1.2 miles) offers a good viewpoint in late fall, winter, and early spring.

At about 2.5 miles come to a series of switchbacks descending the ridge. Reach the bottom and follow the trail as it curves to the right (west) to return to the trailhead.

Miles and Directions

0.0 From the parking area follow the trail northwest passing the old limekiln.

0.3 Cross a shallow stream and continue northwest.

1.0 Cross a drainage and follow the trail as it ascends a moderately steep ridge.

1.2 Reach the bench and viewing area at the top of the ridge.

2.5 Come to the first of a series of switchbacks descending the ridge.

2.8 Return to the trailhead.

9 Castlewood State Park: River Scene Trail

This loop trail offers visitors a steep climb to scenic limestone bluffs and a flat finish through the floodplain along the Meramec River in Castlewood State Park.

Distance: 3.4-mile loop
Approximate hiking time: 1.5 hours
Difficulty: Moderate due to modest climb
Best season: Year-round
Park hours: Open 7 a.m. to half hour after sunset
Other trail users: Mountain bikers allowed on a portion of the trail
Canine compatibility: Leashed dogs permitted

Fees and permits: None
Maps: USGS Manchester; park map available at visitor center
Trail contacts: Castlewood State Park, 1401 Kiefer Creek Rd., Ballwin, MO 63021; (800) 334-6946; www.mostateparks.com /castlewood.htm
Special considerations: Ticks, mosquitoes, and poison ivy are common in warmer months.

Finding the trailhead: From St. Louis take I-44 West for 16.8 miles to exit 272 (MO 141). Merge onto North Highway Drive and then take a slight right onto MO 141 for 1.8 miles. Take the Big Bend Road ramp, staying left on West Big Bend Road. Drive 2.4 miles to Ries Road. Turn left onto Ries Road and travel 1 mile, then turn left onto Kiefer Creek Road into the park. Continue 0.4 mile to the trailhead parking area, picnic shelter, restrooms, and playground on the left (northeast) side of the road. GPS: N38 32.993 / W90 32.371

The Hike

Known as "St. Louis's Peaceful Escape," Castlewood State Park is a popular destination for many outdoor enthusiasts in the area. Hikers, equestrians, and bikers share many of the trails in the park. Anglers and paddlers also use the park as an access point to the Meramec River.

The River Scene Trail showcases some of the finest sights in the park. Limestone bluffs offer good views of the Meramec River. The trail gives visitors a taste of upland forest, consisting of mostly white oak and shagbark hickory, as well as a glimpse of bottomland forest, which includes silver maples, box elders, and sycamore trees.

From the parking area, cross Kiefer Creek Road and locate the signed trailhead for the River Scene Trail to the southwest. Follow the trail to the south as it parallels Kiefer Creek Road before ascending a moderately steep and rocky ridge. As you near the top of the ridge, the Meramec River comes into view to the south. Come to the first of several scenic overlooks at 0.3 mile. At 0.4 mile the trail forks; hikers stay left and mountain bikers go right. Stay left at another fork at 0.5 mile. Avoid the bike trail at 0.7 mile, continuing west on the hiking trail. Shortly after, descend a series of wooden steps and cross a boardwalk at 1.1 miles.

Cross under the railroad tracks at 1.2 miles and follow the trail as it curves to the east. The trail surface at this point alternates between moist sand and dirt, providing excellent opportunities to look for wildlife tracks, such as wild turkey, raccoon, and white-tailed deer. After 2.0 miles come to an intersection with a connector trail; stay right and follow the red arrows to continue on the River Scene Trail. Come to a river access point at 2.8 miles and continue north, passing

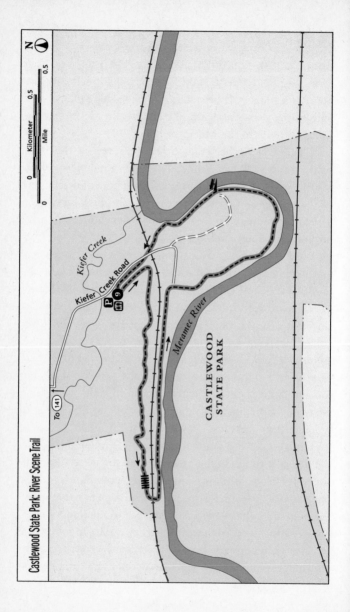

Castlewood State Park: River Scene Trail

N

0   0.5   Kilometer
0   0.5   Mile

Kiefer Creek

Kiefer Creek Road

To 141

P

Meramec River

CASTLEWOOD
STATE PARK

an information kiosk. At 3.2 miles the trail reaches Kiefer Creek Road and crosses under the railroad tracks. Cross Kiefer Creek Road on the north side of the railroad tracks and follow the trail back to the trailhead parking area.

Miles and Directions

0.0 From the signed trailhead turn left and follow the River Scene Trail south.

0.3 Come to the first of several scenic overlooks.

0.4 Hikers stay left at the fork.

0.5 Reach another fork; hikers stay left.

0.7 Avoid the bike trail to the right (north); continue west on hiking trail.

1.1 Come to boardwalk.

1.2 Cross under the railroad tracks and follow the trail as it curves to the east.

2.0 Come to an intersection with a connector trail. Stay right (south), following the red arrows.

2.8 Reach the river access point; continue north on a paved trail.

3.0 Stay right (north) at the fork on the dirt trail.

3.2 Come to Kiefer Creek Road; cross under the railroad tracks, then cross the road. The trail continues to the northwest.

3.4 Return to the trailhead.

10 West Tyson County Park: Flint Quarry Trail

Passing through the Crescent Hills, the Flint Quarry Trail is an ideal destination for hikers hoping to escape the city and enjoy the natural and cultural history of West Tyson County Park.

Distance: 2.5-mile loop

Approximate hiking time: 2 hours

Difficulty: Moderate due to modest climb

Best season: Fall through spring

Park hours: Open 8 a.m. to half hour past official sunset

Other trail users: Portions of the trail open to mountain bikers and equestrians

Canine compatibility: Leashed dogs permitted

Fees and permits: None

Maps: USGS Manchester; St. Louis County Park maps available online

Trail contacts: West Tyson County Park, 131 North Outer Rd. East, Eureka, MO 63025; (636) 938-5144; www.stlouisco.com/parks

Special considerations: Ticks and poison ivy are common in warmer months, and the park is home to copperheads and timber rattlesnakes. For emergencies contact the county park rangers at (314) 615-8911.

Finding the trailhead: From St. Louis take I-44 West to exit 266 (Lewis Road). Turn right onto Lewis Road, which quickly becomes West Outer Road, and drive 0.1 mile. The park entrance is on the right. After entering the park, drive 0.1 mile and stay to the right toward Roth Lodge. Continue 0.2 mile; the road dead-ends at the parking lot and trailhead. Modern restrooms and water are available at the trailhead. GPS: N38 30.678 / W90 35.194

The Hike

The 611-acre West Tyson County Park is a perfect place to visit for hikers looking to escape the crowds found on many of the other, more-popular trails in the area. The park tends to be a little overshadowed by Route 66 State Park, which sits right next door. It does gain some extra traffic from the popular 7.0-mile Chubb Trail, which runs through a portion of the park.

Be on the lookout for wildlife, including white-tailed deer and wild turkey, as you follow the trail up and around the rocky ridge.

A few brief but scenic overlooks can be enjoyed among the forest of oak, hickory, and maple trees.

Named for the numerous flint quarries found in the area, the Flint Quarry Trail loops through West Tyson County Park. As a result of the hundreds of flint quarries found in the park, a portion of the park is on the National Register of Historic Places. Native Americans mined the flint in these hills and shaped it into tools and weapons. The flint knapping occurred in the village floodplains and not at the quarry sites; therefore, no artifacts occur at the flint mines.

From the parking area, follow the paved trail north to the Flint Quarry Trail. The Flint Quarry Trail branches right (northeast) at 0.1 mile. The obvious dirt-and-rock trail ascends a ridge through maples, chinkapin oaks, and cedars.

At 1.4 miles come to the intersection with the Chubb Trail; turn left (southwest) onto that trail. Come to a fork in the trail at 2.2 miles; stay left (south) to continue on the Flint Quarry Trail. At 2.4 miles reach the intersection with the paved walking path. Follow the path south to return to the trailhead parking area.

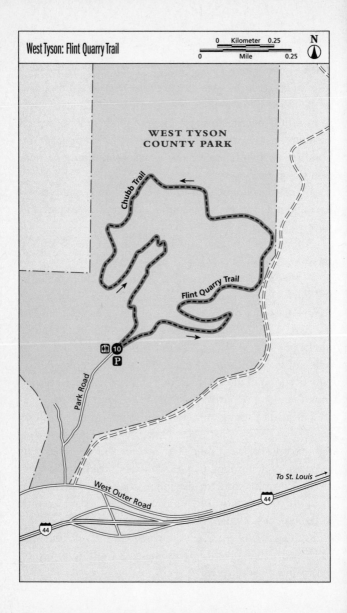

West Tyson: Flint Quarry Trail

0   Kilometer   0.25

0   Mile   0.25

N

WEST TYSON
COUNTY PARK

Chubb Trail

Flint Quarry Trail

10
P

Park Road

West Outer Road

44

To St. Louis →

44

Miles and Directions

0.0 From the parking area begin hiking north on the paved path.

0.1 Turn right (northeast) onto the Flint Quarry Trail, marked with a green quarry symbol.

1.4 Turn left (southwest) onto the Chubb Trail.

2.2 Turn left (south) onto the Flint Quarry Trail.

2.4 Come to the paved walking path; follow it south.

2.5 Return to the trailhead parking area.

11 Lone Elk County Park: White Bison Trail

Herds of elk and buffalo are undoubtedly an uncommon occurrence in St. Louis County, yet a trip to Lone Elk County Park can offer wildlife lovers sightings of both. The White Bison Trail presents wildlife viewing opportunities rarely seen in this part of the country.

Distance: 3.0-mile loop
Approximate hiking time: 2 hours
Difficulty: Moderate due to modest climbs
Best season: Year-round
Park hours: Open 8 a.m. to half hour past official sunset
Other trail users: None
Canine compatibility: No dogs permitted in park or on trails

Fees and permits: None
Maps: USGS Manchester
Trail contacts: Lone Elk County Park, 1 Lone Elk Park Rd., Valley Park, MO 63088; (314) 615-4386, www.stlouisco.com/parks
Special considerations: Ticks and chiggers are common in warmer months.

Finding the trailhead: From St. Louis take I-44 West for 17 miles to exit 272 for MO 141 and merge onto North Highway Drive. Make a slight right onto MO 141 and then take the ramp to North Outer Road. Turn left onto Meramec Street and stay straight onto West Outer Road for 2 miles. Turn right onto Lone Elk Park Road. Drive 0.6 mile to the park entrance on the left, and then drive 0.2 mile more, staying left at the fork. Follow the road for another 0.3 mile to the visitor center, parking area, and trailhead. Modern restrooms and water are available at the visitor center. GPS: N38 31.873 / W90 32.600

The Hike

Lone Elk County Park, an interesting park with a peculiar past, makes a memorable day trip for hikers in and around St. Louis. Part of a large cattle operation in the 1800s, the area that now makes up Lone Elk Park was purchased by the Military Department in 1941 and used as an ammunition depot until the end of World War II. After the war, the area was declared surplus and taken over by St. Louis County Parks.

Taking advantage of the 8-foot-tall perimeter fence, the new park was stocked with ten elk from Yellowstone National Park. In 1951 the park was taken over by the Department of the Army and used once again for military purposes.

By the end of the 1950s the herd had grown to more than one hundred elk, and the animals were beginning to run out of food. With winter approaching, it was decided that all the elk would be exterminated and the meat donated to local hospitals. One lone bull escaped this fate and roamed the hills alone for several years.

In 1963 the area was taken over by Washington University, and in 1966 students from Rockwood School District partnered with the West St. Louis Lions Club to purchase more elk from Yellowstone, bringing the lone elk some much-needed company after eight years of solitude.

Today hikers in Lone Elk County Park can expect to see elk, white-tailed deer, wild turkey, waterfowl, and bison. The forest is a typical Missouri hardwood mix, full of oaks and hickories. Visitors who want to extend their trip can visit the World Bird Sanctuary to see bald eagles, hawks, owls, and more.

The White Bison Trail loops around Lone Elk Reservoir, and hikers will more than likely pass right by the elk

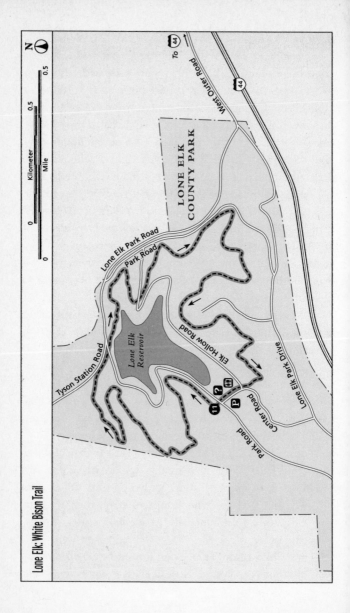

Lone Elk: White Bison Trail

herds that rest near the trail. Visitors will have to enjoy the bison from their vehicles, as the herd is kept separate from the rest of the park.

From the visitor center parking area, locate the White Bison Trail on the west side of Lone Elk Park Road. The trail begins near the picnic area, just across a small footbridge, and is marked with a white buffalo trail marker. The trail ascends a steep, rocky slope and curves northeast through hickories, oaks, maples, and redbuds. The trail passes through a woodland area that includes an abundance of pawpaw trees. The trail bends sharply to the right (north) at 0.9 mile and descends the hill.

Come to a park road at 1.1 miles and turn right (east). Follow the road for 0.1 mile, crossing Lone Elk Park Road and following the trail east into the woods. (The lake will be to the south of the trail.) Cross Elk Hollow Road and a picnic area at 1.6 miles and continue following the trail south.

At 2.0 miles the trail turns to the right (west). Come to another park road at 3.0 miles; the visitor center and trailhead parking are just ahead (west).

Miles and Directions

0.0 From the footbridge begin hiking west.

0.9 The trail bends sharply to the right (north) and descends the hill.

1.1 Come to a park road and turn right (east), following the road up a short hill.

1.2 Cross Lone Elk Park Road and continue east into the woods.

1.6 Cross Elk Hollow Road and a picnic area.

2.0 Follow the trail as it curves to the west.

3.0 Cross a park road and continue west to return to the visitor center.

12 Cliff Cave County Park: Spring Valley Trail

Managed by St. Louis County Parks, Cliff Cave County Park is home to the second-largest cave in St. Louis County. Although the cave itself is closed to protect the endangered Indiana bat, this short loop makes a fine day trip only minutes from the city.

Distance: 2.1-mile loop
Approximate hiking time: 1.5 hours
Difficulty: Moderate due to modest climb
Best season: Fall through spring
Park hours: Open 8 a.m. to half hour past official sunset
Other trail users: Mountain bikers and equestrians
Canine compatibility: Leashed dogs permitted

Fees and permits: None
Maps: USGS Oakville; St. Louis County park maps available online
Trail contacts: Cliff Cave County Park, 806 Cliff Cave Rd., St. Louis, MO 63129; (314) 846-8337; www.co.st-louis.mo.us /parks/CliffCave.html
Special considerations: Ticks are common in warmer months.

Finding the trailhead: From St. Louis take I-55 South for 10 miles to exit 197 (I-255 East). Drive 2.7 miles on I-255 East and take the Telegraph Road exit. Drive 1.9 miles on Telegraph Road to Cliff Cave Road; turn left. Follow Cliff Cave Road for 1.1 miles to the park gate; travel another 0.4 mile to the trailhead and parking on the right. GPS: N38 27.546 / W90 17.461

The Hike

Cliff Cave County Park received the "Best View of the Mississippi" Award in 2009 for a good reason: The Mississippi River provides the entire eastern border of the park. The 525-acre park opened to the public in 1977 after being bought for $400,000 in 1972. The cave was used as a riverside tavern by French traders in the 1700s and as a wine cellar in the 1800s. Today it provides habitat for the endangered Indiana bat.

Hikers enjoy the shade of oaks, hickories, and dogwoods in the forested portions of the park. Visitors who choose to hike along the Mississippi River Trail will encounter beautifully restored wetland prairies that were once very common in these floodplains. The cave itself is closed to visitors, both to protect the rare bat population and to protect the cave itself from vandalism, but if you visit in winter, you can witness the cave "breathing" a cold mist.

The Spring Valley Trail features Indian Cave, also known as Cliff Cave, which hikers can look into at either the start or the end of the hike, as the loop begins and ends here. The trail is one of the more challenging hikes in the park and the most urban. You will pass several social trail intersections that lead to nearby neighborhoods and are used by locals to access the trail.

From the trailhead parking area, locate the Spring Valley Trail sign and follow the arrow west as you walk along Cliff Cave Road. Just before the guardrails, the trail turns to the left and is marked with an orange diamond and blue square. At 0.1 mile cross a shallow creek and follow the trail to the right (north) as it ascends the ridge. Be careful to avoid several unmarked spur trails in this area.

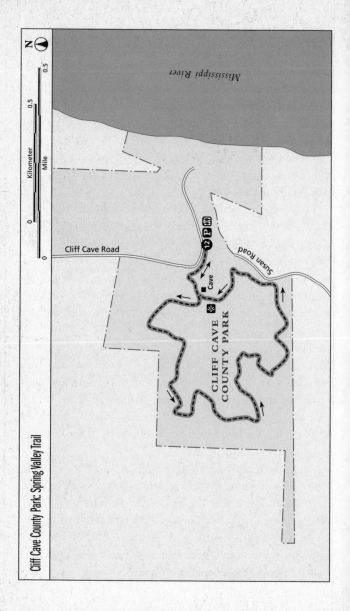

Cliff Cave County Park: Spring Valley Trail

Mississippi River

Cliff Cave Road

12 P

Cave

Susan Road

CLIFF CAVE
COUNTY PARK

N

Kilometer
Mile
0   0.5

0   0.5

At 0.2 mile reach the actual beginning of the loop; stay to the right. You will notice dogwood, shagbark hickory, and sassafras as you meander through the area's karst topography. The trail passes behind several houses as it skirts the edge of a suburb and briefly reminds you that you are in fact only minutes from the city.

At 1.7 miles reach a sign that reads PARK EXIT, SUSAN ROAD ACCESS. Turn left (north) here to stay on the Spring Valley Trail. Reach a sign marking the end/start of the loop at 1.9 miles. Turn right (east) and follow the trail back to Cliff Cave Road and the trailhead parking area.

Miles and Directions

0.0 From the parking area follow Cliff Cave Road west; turn left onto the Spring Valley Trail.

0.1 Cross a creek and follow the trail north, ascending a ridge.

0.2 Come to the beginning of the loop portion of the hike; stay right (north).

1.7 Come to the spur trail signed PARK EXIT, SUSAN ROAD ACCESS. Turn left (north) to stay on Spring Valley Trail.

1.9 Reach the end of the loop portion of the hike. Turn right (east) to return to the trailhead and parking area.

2.1 Arrive back at the trailhead and parking area.

13 St. Francois State Park: Mooner's Hollow Trail

This area was once a popular spot for moonshine production. The loop trail follows the cold, clear waters of Coonville Creek through a lovely mixed-hardwood forest.

Distance: 3.0-mile loop
Approximate hiking time: 1.5 hours
Difficulty: Moderate due to modest climbs
Best season: Fall through spring
Park hours: Apr–Oct, 7 a.m.–10 p.m.; Nov–Mar, 8 a.m.–6 p.m.
Other trail users: None
Canine compatibility: Leashed dogs permitted

Fees and permits: None
Maps: USGS Bonne Terre
Trail contacts: St. Francois State Park, 8920 US 67 North, Bonne Terre, MO 63628; (573) 358-2173; www.mostateparks.com /stfrancois.htm; e-mail: moparks @dnr.mo.gov
Special considerations: Ticks and poison ivy are common in warmer weather.

Finding the trailhead: From St. Louis take I-55 South for 33 miles to exit 174B (US 67 South). Follow US 67 South for 19.3 miles before turning left onto Park Road. Drive 0.4 mile on Park Road to the parking area and trailhead on the left. GPS: N37 58.212 / W90 31.992

The Hike

The first acres of St. Francois State Park were purchased in 1964 in an effort to preserve the history and beauty of the area. The 2,101 acres of Coonville Creek Wild Area provided hideouts during the Civil War as well as during

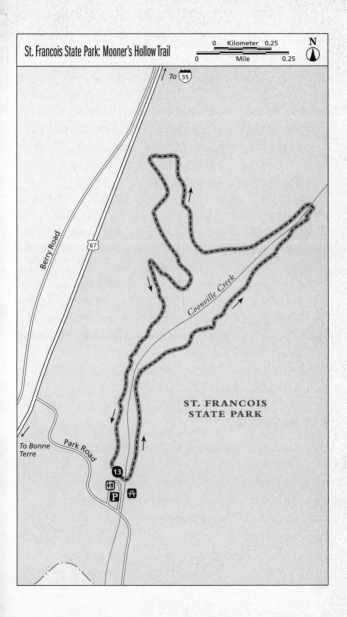

St. Francois State Park: Mooner's Hollow Trail

0   Kilometer   0.25

0   Mile   0.25

N

To 55

Berry Road

67

Coonville Creek

ST. FRANCOIS
STATE PARK

To Bonne
Terre

Park Road

13

P

Prohibition. Today the park totals 2,735 acres and still offers a retreat for visitors looking to get away from the city.

Hikers, boaters, and campers all make their way to St. Francois State Park on a regular basis. The Big River, at the southern boundary of the park, offers beautiful canoeing opportunities. The 110 campsites offer ample space to pitch a tent, take a shower, and even do some laundry. Over 16 miles of hiking trails provide plenty of space to get away from the crowds and enjoy nature.

Mooner's Hollow Trail is named for the moonshining activities that took place in the hollow. The trail travels along Coonville Creek and then up along a rugged ridge-line. Hikers pass through several glades that offer some brief scenic views and plenty of wildflowers.

From the parking area, locate the information kiosk and trailhead. Cross Coonville Creek and begin hiking northeast, following the obvious trail and blue trail markers. The trail follows Coonville Creek and crosses it at 1.1 miles, then turns to the northwest.

After 2.5 miles cross a shallow tributary and continue southwest to the trailhead parking area.

Miles and Directions

0.0 From the trailhead cross a footbridge and begin hiking northeast.

1.1 Cross Coonville Creek and turn northwest.

2.5 Cross a shallow tributary; continue hiking southwest.

3.0 Return to the trailhead parking area.

14 Pickle Springs Natural Area: Trail through Time

A highlight of the Pickle Springs Natural Area, this short interpretive hike features towering limestone bluffs, breezy canyons, and several interesting rock formations.

Distance: 2.0-mile loop
Approximate hiking time: 1 to 2 hours
Difficulty: Moderate due to modest climb
Best season: Year-round
Other trail users: None
Park hours: Open sunrise to half hour after sunset
Canine compatibility: Leashed dogs permitted
Fees and permits: None
Maps: USGS Sprott; interpretive trail guide available at the information kiosk
Trail contacts: Pickle Springs Natural Area, 2302 County Park Dr., Cape Girardeau, MO 63701; (573) 290-5730; http://mdc.mo .gov/discover-nature/places-go /natural-areas/pickle-springs
Special considerations: Ticks and poison ivy are common in warmer months. Use caution near bluffs.

Finding the trailhead: From St. Louis take I-55 South for 57 miles to exit 150 (MO 32 West). Follow MO 32 West from the junction with I-55 past Hawn State Park to MO AA. Turn left onto MO AA and drive about 1 mile to Dorlac Road. Turn left and follow gravel Dorlac Road about 0.5 mile to the parking lot and the trailhead located on the right. GPS: N37 48.083 / W90 18.087

The Hike

Pickle Springs Natural Area was named for William Pickles, an Illinois settler in the 1850s. As more has been learned about the area, it has received more and more recognition. The state natural area was designated a National Natural Landmark in 1974.

Researchers believe that mammoths once roamed the canyons grazing on plants like northern white violets, orchids, and cinnamon ferns. All of these plants can still be found in Pickle Springs Natural Area. It tends to be the geology that keeps visitors coming back though, and the Trail through Time highlights some of the area's most unusual rock formations. The Lamotte sandstone has made its way from the bottom of ancient seas to expose rock formations not typically seen in Missouri.

The interpretive trail has been designed to lead hikers through all the area's amazing sites. Hikers have the opportunity to enjoy beautiful rock formations, cool box canyons, and a lush forest. Some visitors will find that the hike takes longer than usual because of all the sites.

From the parking area, begin hiking east on the obvious and well-maintained mulch-covered trail. At 0.1 mile come to the information kiosk; the kiosk is stocked with trail maps and an interpretive pamphlet that corresponds to many of the sites along the trail. The loop begins at the kiosk; turn left (north) to continue on the one-way trail.

Reach "The Slot" at 0.2 mile; turn right (east) and cross through the tight walls of Lamotte sandstone. Come to the interesting rock formations known as Cauliflower Rocks and Double Arch at 0.4 mile. At 0.6 mile cross to a wooden footbridge and continue northeast across Pickle Creek.

Come to the bluff shelter known as Spirit Canyon at 1.0 mile; follow the trail as it curves to the right (west). Cross Pickle Creek again at 1.5 miles and continue west. At 1.7 miles reach Piney Glade, a sandstone glade, near the top

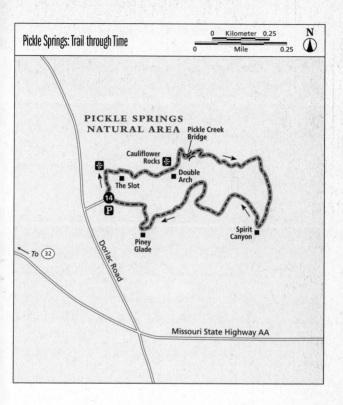

Pickle Springs: Trail through Time

PICKLE SPRINGS
NATURAL AREA

Pickle Creek
Bridge

Cauliflower
Rocks

Double
Arch

The Slot

14
P

Piney
Glade

Spirit
Canyon

To 32

Doriac Road

Missouri State Highway AA

of the ridge; follow the trail as it curves to the northwest. Return to the information kiosk at 1.9 miles; turn left (west) and return to the parking area.

Miles and Directions

0.0 Begin hiking east on the obvious, mulch-covered trail.

0.1 Turn left (north) at the information kiosk.

0.2 Pass through The Slot.

0.4 Pass by Cauliflower Rock and through Double Arch.

0.6 Cross Pickle Creek and continue northeast.

1.0 Come to Spirit Canyon and begin heading west.

1.5 Cross Pickle Creek again and continue west.

1.7 Reach Piney Glade and follow the trail as it curves to the northeast.

1.9 Return to the information kiosk; turn left (west).

2.0 Arrive back at the trailhead parking area.

15 Hawn State Park: White Oaks Trail

Winding through a mixed hardwood forest, the White Oaks Trail features mature white oaks and lofty shortleaf pines, as well as unusual outcroppings of Lamotte sandstone.

Distance: 4.1-mile lollipop
Approximate hiking time: 2 to 3 hours
Difficulty: Moderate due to length
Best season: Year-round
Park hours: Open Mar 15–Nov 15, 7:30 a.m.–9 p.m.; Nov 15–Mar 14, 7:30 to sunset
Other trail users: None
Canine compatibility: Leashed dogs permitted

Fees and permits: None
Maps: USGS Coffman Quad; trail maps available at the visitor center
Trail contacts: Hawn State Park, 12096 Park Dr., Ste. Genevieve, MO 63670; (573) 883-3603; www.mostateparks.com /hawn.htm
Special considerations: Ticks and chiggers are abundant from early summer through mid-fall.

Finding the trailhead: From St. Louis take I-55 South to exit 150. Turn right onto MO 32 and drive toward the town of Farmington. After 11 miles, turn left onto MO 144 and drive south for 3 miles to the Hawn State Park entrance. At the park entrance, turn right into the White Oaks Trail parking area. GPS: N37 49.997 / W90 14.415

The Hike

Containing some of the most scenic views in the state, Hawn State Park offers a wonderfully diverse natural landscape with canyon-rimmed valleys, clear sand–bottom streams, and mixed oak-pine forests. Large stands of mature shortleaf pine, Missouri's only native pine species, are one of the park's many highlights that can be easily enjoyed

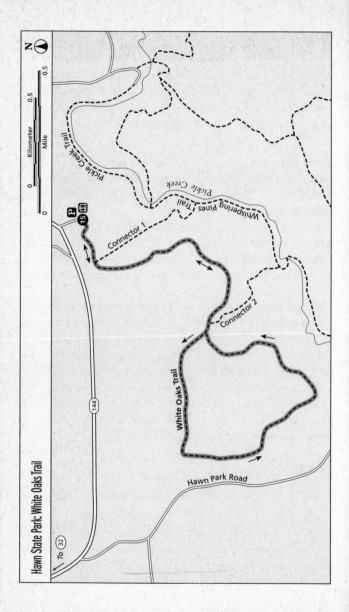

Hawn State Park: White Oaks Trail

from the White Oaks Trail. Another natural jewel of this hike is the Lamotte sandstone. This ancient coarse-grained sandstone has the ability to hold groundwater and produces a variety of distinctive flowers and plants.

From the parking area, locate the trailhead register and information kiosk. Follow the obvious and well-marked White Oaks Trail west as it gradually descends through a shortleaf pine forest before crossing a small, shallow creek. Shortly after you cross this creek, Connector Trail 1 branches to the left (southeast). This trail, marked with a yellow arrow, takes you to the Whispering Pines Trail. Continue straight (west) to stay on the White Oaks Trail as it crosses another shallow creek and heads up a mellow ridge through a mixed-hardwood forest and Lamotte sandstone outcroppings.

After 1.1 miles, Connector Trail 2 branches to the left (southeast); keep right. Follow the sign pointing toward the White Oaks Trail and cross another shallow creek. Soon come to a sign that reads WHITE OAKS TRAIL LOOP 1.8 MILES with an arrow pointing to the right. Follow this loop trail north then west as it follows the sandy drainage, where wildlife tracks are easily visible.

Complete the loop portion of the hike at 2.9 miles. Turn right and backtrack to the trailhead.

Miles and Directions

0.0 Leave the parking area and begin hiking west on the White Oaks Trail.

0.2 Connector Trail 1 branches to the left (southeast); continue straight on the White Oaks Trail.

1.1 Connector Trail 2 branches to the left (southeast); follow the signs pointing toward the White Oaks Trail.

1.2 Reach the beginning of the White Oaks Trail loop and bear right (northwest).

2.9 Come to the end of the White Oaks Trail loop; turn right (east) and retrace your steps to the trailhead.

4.1 Return to the trailhead.

16 Hawn State Park: Whispering Pines Trail–North Loop

Traversing a mixed-hardwood and pine forest, the north loop of the Whispering Pines Trail offers a longer day trip for hikers looking to take in many of the sites in Hawn State Park.

Distance: 6.5-mile loop
Approximate hiking time: 4 hours
Difficulty: More challenging due to length and some challenging climbs
Best season: Fall through spring
Park hours: Open Mar 15–Nov 14, 7:30 a.m.–9 p.m.; Nov 15–Mar 14, 7:30 to sunset
Other trail users: None
Canine compatibility: Leashed dogs permitted

Fees and permits: None
Maps: USGS Coffman; trail maps available at the visitor center
Trail contacts: Hawn State Park, 12096 Park Dr., Ste. Genevieve, MO 63670; (573) 883-3603; www.mostateparks.com/hawn.htm; e-mail: moparks@dnr.mo.gov
Special considerations: Ticks and poison ivy are common in warmer months.

Finding the trailhead: From St. Louis take I-55 South for 57 miles to exit 150 (MO 32 West). Follow MO 32 West from the junction with I-55 for 11.3 miles to MO 144. Turn left onto MO 144 and follow the road for 2.9 miles to the park entrance. At the stop sign, turn left onto Park Drive and continue 1.1 miles to a fork. Stay right at the fork and drive 0.1 mile to the parking area and trailhead on the left. GPS: N37 49.760 / W90 13.811

The Hike

Many visitors to Hawn State Park believe it to be the loveliest park in Missouri. The 4,953-acre park is located in the eastern Ozark Mountains and is home to the 2,880-acre Whispering Pines Wild Area and Pickle Creek, a state natural area. The park was acquired by the state in 1955.

The area is believed to have been part of a large, sandy floodplain that stretched as far north as Canada around 600 million years ago. Through cycles of uplift and erosion, the sandstone cliffs and bluffs are all that remain. Today hikers can enjoy rich shortleaf pine forests, mixed oak and maple trees, and plenty of flowering dogwoods. The park is also popular with rock hounds and bird-watchers.

If it's a windy day, you'll soon understand why the trail is called the Whispering Pines Trail. Many people say it sounds like the pine trees are actually whispering to you as the wind blows through them. For an extended day hike or even a short overnight backpack trip, the north loop can be combined with the south loop for a 10.0-mile hike.

From the parking area, locate the Whispering Pines Trail to the south. A sign marks the trail at the trailhead, and hikers are encouraged to sign the trailhead register.

Cross the wooden footbridge and continue hiking south to cross a second wooden footbridge at 0.1 mile. Turn right here and follow the red directional arrow southwest. Come to a fork in the trail at 0.3 mile; stay right (southwest) to stay on the Whispering Pines Trail–North Loop.

Wade across the babbling Pickle Creek at 1.0 mile and turn left (west). Intersect Connector Trail 1, which connects to the White Oaks Trail, at 1.3 miles. Stay left and continue hiking southwest on the Whispering Pines Trail–North Loop. At 1.8 miles intersect Connector Trail 2, which also connects to the White Oaks Trail. Stay left and continue southwest.

At 3.2 miles come to Connector Trail 3 on the left (north) side of the trail. This connector leads to a primitive camping area and can be used to shorten this hike, as it eventually leads to the trailhead parking area. Stay right (east) to continue on the Whispering Pines Trail–North Loop.

At 3.7 miles reach the junction of the north and south loops of the Whispering Pines Trail. Stay to the left (northeast) to continue on the north loop. In another 0.1 mile come to a second junction with the south loop. Again stay left (north) to continue on the north loop and return to the trailhead.

Reach Pickle Creek at 5.4 miles; follow the trail as it turns to the left (southwest). Return to the footbridge at 6.4 miles. Turn right (north) to cross the bridge and return to the trailhead parking area.

Miles and Directions

0.0 Begin hiking south, crossing a wooden footbridge.

0.1 Cross a second wooden footbridge and then turn right (southwest).

0.3 Stay right at the fork and continue southwest.

1.0 Cross Pickle Creek; turn left (west).

1.3 Intersect Connector Trail 1; stay straight (southwest) to continue on main trail.

1.8 Intersect Connector Trail 2; stay straight (southwest) to continue on the main trail.

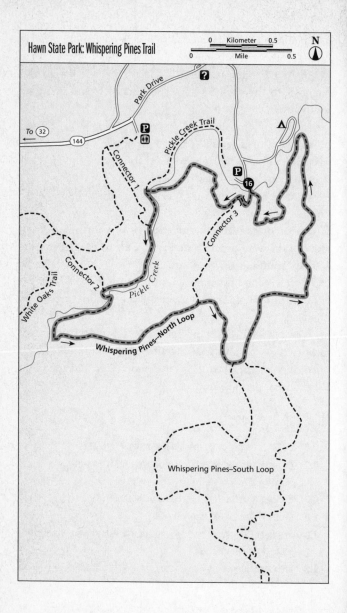

Kilometer
0   0.5

Mile
0   0.5

N

Park Drive

To 32

144

Pickle Creek Trail

P

16

Connector 1

Connector 2

Connector 3

White Oaks Trail

Pickle Creek

Whispering Pines–North Loop

Whispering Pines–South Loop

3.2 Intersect Connector Trail 3; continue east on the main trail. (**Option:** Turn left onto the connector to return to the trail-head for a shorter hike.)

3.7 Intersect the Whispering Pines Trail–South Loop. Continue northeast on the north loop.

3.8 Stay left (north) at the second junction with the Whispering Pines Trail–South Loop.

5.4 Come to Pickle Creek; the trail turns to the left (southwest).

6.4 Return to a wooden footbridge. Turn right (north) to cross the bridge and return to the trailhead parking area.

6.5 Return to the trailhead.

17 Mastodon State Historic Site: Limestone Hill Trail

The longest trail in Mastodon State Historic Site, the Limestone Hill Trail offers a rugged but scenic hike that traverses the base of an interesting limestone bluff.

Distance: 2.0-mile loop
Approximate hiking time: 1.5 hours
Difficulty: Moderate due to modest climb
Best season: Fall through spring
Park hours: Open 8 a.m. to half hour past sunset
Other trail users: None
Canine compatibility: Leashed dogs permitted
Fees and permits: None

Maps: USGS Lake Killarney; trail map available at visitor center
Trail contacts: Mastodon State Historic Site, 1050 Museum Dr., Imperial, MO 63052; (636) 464-2976; www.mostateparks.com /mastodon.htm
Special considerations: Ticks and poison ivy are common during warmer weather. Use caution when crossing Seckman Road.

Finding the trailhead: From St. Louis take I-55 South for 20.7 miles to exit 186 (Imperial Main Street). Turn right onto Imperial Main Street and then make an immediate right onto West Outer Road. Drive 0.6 mile on West Outer Road to a stop sign; turn left onto Seckman Road. Follow Seckman Road for 0.8 mile into the park and to the parking area on the left. GPS: N38 22.821 / W90 23.690

The Hike

The bones of ancient mastodons were found here in the early 1800s. The Kimmswick Bone Bed, a Pleistocene epoch deposit, quickly gained fame among scientists from around the world. In 1979 a stone spear point 10,000 to 14,000 years old was excavated, confirming the existence of humans and mastodons in the same time period.

The 431-acre Mastodon State Historic Site offers three hiking trails. Hikes range from short and simple strolls along the bone beds and the Callison Memorial Bird Sanctuary to the longer Limestone Hill Trail. Hikers can expect the usual mixed-hardwood forests of oak, hickory, and maple trees. For a small entry fee, you can visit the museum to view mastodon fossils, bones, and other artifacts.

The Limestone Hill Trail begins at the only picnic site in the small park. This loop is the longest and most challenging hike in the park. The Limestone Hill and Spring Branch Trails share the same trailhead and can be easily combined to extend your hike by 0.75 mile.

From the north end of the parking area, locate the information kiosk and trailhead marker. Follow the obvious gravel trail and the trail markers for Limestone Hill Trail west and then north to cross Seckman Road (0.1 mile). On the other side of Seckman Road, turn left (west) and follow the trail as in parallel Seckman Road.

At 0.3 mile the trail curves to the right (north) and ascends the hill to a bench and scenic overlook at 0.7 mile. Stay right to avoid a spur trail and continue southeast on the Limestone Hill Trail.

At 1.2 miles come to another fork in the trail. Stay right and follow the trail marker, which points south, down a gradual hill. Return to Seckman Road at 1.9 miles. Cross the road and continue south to the trailhead parking area.

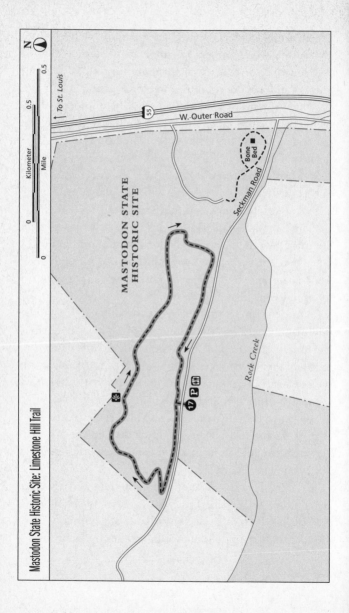

Mastodon State Historic Site: Limestone Hill Trail

Miles and Directions

0.0 From the trailhead begin hiking west then north toward Seckman Road.

0.1 Cross Seckman Road and turn left (west).

0.3 Follow the trail as it curves to the right (north) and ascends a hill.

0.7 Come to a bench and scenic overlook. Keep right to avoid a spur trail.

1.2 Stay right at the fork to continue on the Limestone Hill Trail.

1.9 Cross Seckman Road and continue south.

2.0 Return to trailhead.

18 Piney Creek Ravine Trail

Featuring the largest concentration of prehistoric rock art in Illinois, Piney Creek Trail offers visitors a pleasant day hike rich in both natural and cultural history.

Distance: 2.0-mile lollipop
Approximate hiking time: 1.5 hours
Difficulty: Moderate due to modest climb
Best season: Fall through spring
Park hours: Open sunrise to sunset
Other trail users: None
Canine compatibility: Leashed dogs permitted

Fees and permits: None
Maps: USGS Welge
Trail contacts: Piney Creek Ravine, 4301 South Lake Dr., Chester, IL 62233; (618) 826-2706; http://dnr.state.il.us /lands/landmgt/parks/r4/pcr .htm; e-mail: dnr.randolph county@illinois.gov
Special considerations: Ticks are common in warmer months.

Finding the trailhead: From St. Louis take I-55 South to I-255 East toward Illinois. Cross the Jefferson Barracks Bridge into Illinois and continue 5 miles to the IL 3 exit. Take IL 3 South for 48 miles through Columbia, Waterloo, Red Bud, Ruma, Ellis Grove, and Chester. Ten miles southeast of Chester, a large brown sign for Piney Creek Ravine directs you to turn left onto Hog Hill Road. Follow Hog Hill Road to Piney Creek Road. GPS: N37 53.426 / W89 38.292

The Hike

In 1972 the Illinois Department of Natural Resources purchased the 198-acre area known as Piney Creek Ravine. Now a state natural area and National Natural Landmark, Piney Creek is well known in the area for its rare plant species and its abundance of "rock art," which is believed to date back to the Late Woodland (A.D. 500–1000) and Mississippian (A.D. 1000–1550) eras.

Piney Creek Ravine is one of only two places in Illinois where shortleaf pines grow naturally. The ravine forms a moist, sheltered habitat for mosses and liverworts to grow but also offers dry, exposed bluffs perfect for post and blackjack oaks. Hikers in Piney Creek Ravine may encounter opossums, cottontails, chipmunks, white-tailed deer, fence lizards, rough green snakes, and copperhead snakes. Timber rattlesnakes have never been reported but are a possibility in the area.

Piney Creek Trail begins in a field of all places. Hikers will quickly find themselves entering the ravine after a short walk through the field. Many visitors will find that the 2.0 miles takes longer than anticipated once they begin exploring the area with its numerous petroglyphs and pictographs. You will also find an abundance of "graffiti" in this area, some of which dates back to early settlers and some much more recent.

From the small parking area, locate the information kiosk and begin hiking north on an access lane. Following the fenceline, continue on this grassy path until you reach an interpretive sign at 0.3 mile. At this point follow the dirt trail, marked with a hiker symbol and an arrow, east down a small hill and into a grove of cedar trees.

At 0.5 mile the trail forks; stay left and follow the sign, which points the way to the rock art. Shortly after, the trail turns to the left (west) and crosses the shallow creek. Carefully look for the trail on the other side of the creek and continue west. Very shortly come to another fork in the trail at 0.6 mile. Follow the spur trail to the right to view the rock art.

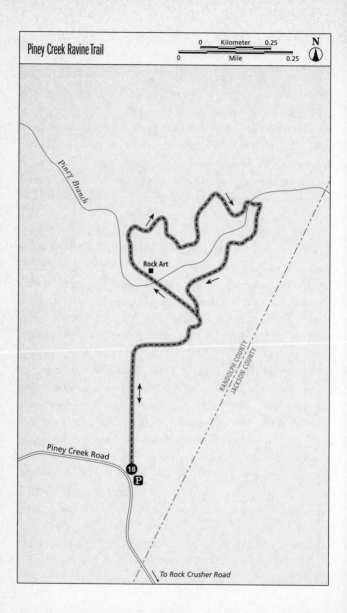

Piney Creek Ravine Trail

0 Kilometer 0.25
0 Mile 0.25

N

Piney Branch

Rock Art

RANDOLPH COUNTY
JACKSON COUNTY

Piney Creek Road

18
P

To Rock Crusher Road

After viewing the petroglyphs and pictographs, return to the main trail and turn right (west). At 1.0 mile follow the trail as it descends through shortleaf pines to a creek. Cross the creek and continue east, reaching the end of the loop at 1.5 miles. Turn left and retrace your steps to the parking area.

Miles and Directions

0.0 Begin hiking north along the grassy access lane.

0.3 Reach the interpretive sign and follow the trail east.

0.5 Stay left (northwest) at the fork; shortly after, turn left (west) and cross the shallow creek.

0.6 Take the spur trail to the right (east) to view the rock art; return to the main trail to continue the hike.

1.0 The trail descends through shortleaf pines.

1.1 Cross a creek.

1.5 Reach the end of the loop. Turn left (south) and retrace your steps to the trailhead.

2.0 Arrive back at the trailhead.

19 Shawnee National Forest: Little Grand Canyon Trail

This loop hike in the Shawnee National Forest features exposed bluffs, an erosion-carved canyon, a seasonal waterfall, and several rock overhangs, making it one of the most interesting trails in the entire region.

Distance: 3.0-mile loop
Approximate hiking time: 2 hours
Difficulty: More challenging due to steep climbs and slippery rocks
Best season: Fall through spring
Park hours: Open 24 hours
Other trail users: None
Canine compatibility: Leashed dogs permitted
Fees and permits: None

Maps: USGS Gorham
Trail contacts: Shawnee National Forest, 50 Hwy. 145 South, Harrisburg, IL 62946; (618) 253-7114
Special considerations: Ticks, mosquitoes, and poison ivy are common during warmer months. Rocks along the trail can be quite slippery following wet weather.

Finding the trailhead: From St. Louis take I-55 South to I-255 East toward Illinois. Cross the Jefferson Barracks Bridge into Illinois and continue 5 miles to the IL 3 exit. Take IL 3 South for 73 miles through Columbia, Waterloo, Red Bud, Ruma, Ellis Grove, and Chester. Turn left onto Town Creek Road and travel 6.6 miles to Hickory Ridge Road. Turn right onto Hickory Ridge Road and continue 4 miles to a four-way stop; turn right to stay on Hickory Ridge Road. Drive 2.3 miles and turn right onto Little Grand Canyon Road. Follow Little Grand Canyon Road until it dead-ends in the parking area. The trailhead is located at the southwest corner of the parking area. GPS: N37 40.842 / W89 23.719

The Hike

A National Natural Landmark, the Little Grand Canyon is a small but dramatic part of the 280,000-acre Shawnee National Forest. Located in Jackson County, Illinois, the deep box canyon has been slowly eroding over time to expose its majestic bluffs.

Visitors to the Little Grand Canyon area will witness typical southern Illinois landscapes. Rich oak and hickory forests tower above sycamore and beech trees. Just south of Little Grand Canyon is a place known as "snake road." Each year the road is closed to accommodate several species of snakes, including timber rattlesnakes, western cottonmouths, and the endangered green water snake, as they migrate to and from their winter hibernation spots.

The Little Grand Canyon Trail begins with a roller coaster–like ridge descent to a scenic overlook. Hikers can stop, enjoy the view, and either return to the parking lot or continue into the canyon below.

The trailhead is located at the southwest corner of the parking area, just to the right (west) of the outhouses. Begin hiking southwest on the obvious gravel-and-dirt trail. Follow the trail as it traverses Viney Ridge through a thick forest of maple, oak, sassafras, beach, and tulip trees.

Pass several wooden benches before reaching a large scenic overlook on Chalk Bluff at 1.2 miles. Here you have a good view of the Big Muddy River to the west. At this point, the trail curves to the right (southeast) and begins to gradually descend the ridge. At 1.4 miles the trail grows noticeable steeper and you enter the moss-covered

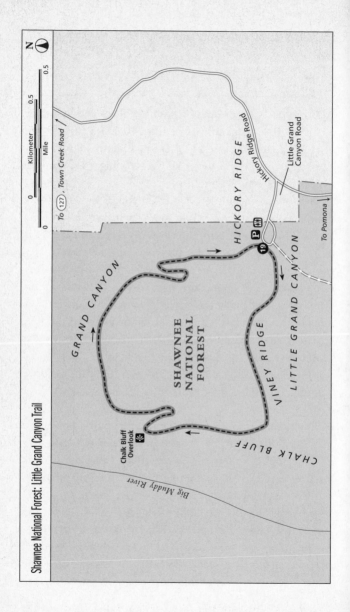

Shawnee National Forest: Little Grand Canyon Trail

sandstone canyon. Carefully descend, alternating between following the trail and the natural drainage. Look closely and you will notice that steps have been etched into the rock in several areas—a work project completed by the Civilian Conservation Corps (CCC) in the 1930s.

At 1.8 miles reach the bottom of the canyon and begin following the trail, now marked with white diamonds, to the east. Cross a small creek at 2.1 miles and continue east, passing tall bluffs. At 2.4 miles the trail curves to right (south) and enters another slippery sandstone drainage. Follow the drainage, again using caution and looking for steps as you pass over several small, seasonal waterfalls.

At the top of the drainage, turn left (east) and ascend the moderately steep trail back to the parking area.

Miles and Directions

0.0   From the trailhead turn left and begin hiking southwest along Viney Ridge.

1.2   Come to the scenic overlook at Chalk Bluff.

1.4   Descend the slippery sandstone canyon.

1.8   Reach the bottom of the canyon and begin hiking east.

2.1   Cross a small creek and continue hiking east.

2.4   Come to the second sandstone canyon and carefully ascend, hiking south. At the top of the drainage, turn left (east) onto the obvious dirt trail.

3.0   Return to the parking area.

20 Shawnee National Forest: Panther Den Trail

A short stroll in the Shawnee National Forest, Panther Den Trail provides easy access to one of the area's most interesting rock formations.

Distance: 2.0 miles out and back

Approximate hiking time: 1 hour

Difficulty: Easy due to length and relatively flat terrain

Best season: Fall through spring

Park hours: 24-hour trail access

Other trail users: Equestrians

Canine compatibility: Leashed dogs permitted

Fees and permits: None

Maps: USGS Lick Creek

Trail contacts: Shawnee National Forest, 50 Hwy. 145 South, Harrisburg, IL 62946; (618) 253-7114

Special considerations: Poison ivy and ticks are common in warmer months.

Finding the trailhead: From St. Louis take I-64 East for 78 miles to I-57 South. Follow I-57 South for 38.5 miles to exit 54B for IL 13 West toward Carbondale. Drive 15 miles into the city of Carbondale. Turn left onto Giant City Road and continue for 7 miles to Grassy Road. Turn left onto Grassy Road and drive 3 miles before turning right onto Rocky Comfort Road. Follow Rocky Comfort Road (staying right at 1.9 miles at the Y) for 4.1 miles to Panthers Den Road. Turn left and drive 1.5 miles to Panthers Den Lane. Turn left again and drive 0.6 mile down the gravel road to the parking area and trailhead on the right. GPS: N37 34.782 / W89 5.295

The Hike

In 1990 the U.S. Congress designated southern Illinois's Panther Den as a wilderness area. Panther Den Wilderness Area totals 1,195 acres. The Shawnee National Forest manages 1,081 acres of the area; the Crab Orchard National Wildlife Refuge manages the remaining acres.

Although the 160-mile River-to-River Trail that runs through Panther Den Wilderness Area receives the most recognition, the several trails that support and branch off the River-to-River Trail offer some amazing opportunities. Hikers choosing Panther Den Trail will traverse an area once believed to have been a large waterway, which over time created a "hiker's playground."

Panther Den Trail is a quick out-and-back hike that leaves plenty of time to explore a remarkable maze of 70-foot-high cliffs. Huge blocks have split off from these cliffs to create a network of crevices, passageways, and cave-like "rooms."

From the parking area, locate the information kiosk and trailhead. Begin hiking northeast on the obvious dirt trail, which is marked with white diamonds. At 0.3 mile a trail branches to the right; continue on Panther Den Trail (Forest Service Trail 371). Soon after, you will pass a fire ring/ camping area on the left (west).

At 0.4 mile cross the creek and continue hiking northeast. At 0.7 mile cross the creek again and enter Panther Den Wilderness Area. Just after entering the wilderness area, come to a fork in the trail and bear left (northeast).

Reach Panther Den at 1.0 mile; explore the many spur trails that lead through the labyrinth of rocks and cliffs.

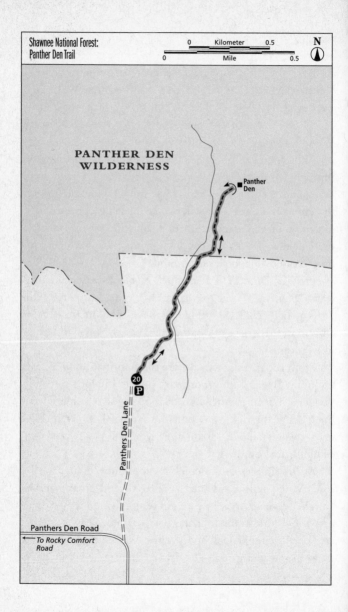

0   Kilometer   0.5

0   Mile   0.5

N

PANTHER DEN
WILDERNESS

■ Panther
Den

20
P

Panthers Den Lane

Panthers Den Road

← To Rocky Comfort
Road

When you are through exploring, return to the trailhead via the same route.

Miles and Directions

0.0 From the trailhead hike northeast on the obvious dirt trail.

0.3 A spur trail forks to the right; continue straight (northeast) to stay on the main trail.

0.4 Cross a creek and continue hiking northeast.

0.7 Enter Panther Den Wilderness Area and bear left (northeast) at the fork.

1.0 Reach Panther Den. After exploring the area, retrace your steps to the trailhead.

2.0 Return to the parking area.

About the Authors

JD Tanner grew up playing and exploring in the hills of southern Illinois. He earned a degree in Outdoor Recreation from Southeast Missouri State University and an advanced degree in Outdoor Recreation from Southern Illinois University in Carbondale. He has traveled extensively throughout the United States and is the Coordinator of Outdoor Recreation at San Juan College in Farmington, New Mexico.

Emily Ressler grew up splitting time between southeast Missouri and southeastern Idaho. She spent her early years fishing, hiking, and camping with her family. In college she enjoyed trying out many new outdoor activities and eventually graduated from Southern Illinois University with an advanced degree in Recreation Resource Administration. She is a third-, fourth-, and fifth-grade teacher at Mosaic Academy in Aztec, New Mexico.

Together they have climbed, hiked, paddled, and camped all over the United States. They co-instructed college-level outdoor recreation courses for several years (and are doing so again) before joining the staff at the Leave No Trace Center for Outdoor Ethics as Traveling Trainers. JD and Emily have written revisions for two FalconGuides: *Best Easy Day Hikes Grand Staircase–Escalante* and *Hiking Grand Staircase–Escalante*. They currently reside in northwestern New Mexico.

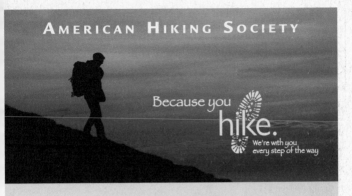

AMERICAN HIKING SOCIETY

Because you hike.

We're with you
every step of the way

American Hiking Society gives voice to the more than 75 million Americans who hike and is the only national organization that promotes and protects foot trails, the natural areas that surround them, and the hiking experience. Our work is inspiring and challenging, and is built on three pillars:

Volunteerism and Stewardship
We organize and coordinate nationally recognized programs—including Volunteer Vacations, National Trails Day ®, and the National Trails Fund—that help keep our trails open, safe, and enjoyable.

Policy and Advocacy
We work with Congress and federal agencies to ensure funding for trails, the preservation of natural areas, and the protection of the hiking experience.

Outreach and Education
We expand and support the national constituency of hikers through outreach and education as well as partnerships with other recreation and conservation organizations.

Join us in our efforts. Become an American Hiking Society member today!

American Hiking Society

1422 Fenwick Lane · Silver Spring, MD 20910 · (800) 972-8608
www.AmericanHiking.org · info@AmericanHiking.org